Collins *gem*

Scots
Dictionary

D0187916

HarperCollins Publishers
Westerhill Road
Bishopbriggs
Glasgow
G64 2QT
Great Britain

First Edition 1995

First published in this
format 2003

Reprint 10 9 8 7 6 5 4

© HarperCollins Publishers 1995

ISBN 978-0-00-722412-8

Collins Gem® and Bank of
English® are registered
trademarks of HarperCollins
Publishers Limited

www.collinslanguage.com

A catalogue record for this book is
available from the British Library

Typeset by
Davidson Pre-Press, Glasgow

Printed in Italy by LEGO Spa, Lavis
(Trento)

Acknowledgements
We would like to thank those
authors and publishers who
kindly gave permission for
copyright material to be used in
the Collins Word Web. We would
also like to thank Times
Newspapers Ltd for providing
valuable data.

Mixed Sources
Product group from well-managed
forests and other controlled sources
www.fsc.org Cert no. SW-COC-1806
© 1996 Forest Stewardship Council

FSC is a non-profit international organisation established to promote the
responsible management of the world's forests. Products carrying the FSC
label are independently certified to assure consumers that they come
from forests that are managed to meet the social, economic and
ecological needs of present and future generations.

Find out more about HarperCollins and the environment at
www.harpercollins.co.uk/green

Contents

EDITORIAL STAFF

INTRODUCTION

About this Book

The Collins Scots Gem is a dictionary of living Scots; but both "living" and "Scots" are terms which need some clarification. By "living" we mean that the words and terms defined are either in current everyday spoken or written use, or are readily familiar to Scottish people.

By "Scots" we mean the language of Germanic origin spoken by most Scots which is neither standard British English or general slang.

Over the years, a great deal of excellent lexicographical work has been done on literary and historical Scots; and in recent years a number of smaller scale dictionaries dealing with the contemporary speech of various regions of Scotland have appeared. The aim of this book is to survey the modern colloquial language of Scotland as a whole, while not neglecting vital archaic or formal terms.

What is in this Dictionary?

This book covers three main types of vocabulary: everyday language, official and technical language, and literary language.

Everyday language. This consists of the words and phrases which people use in normal informal conversation. Some of these are used almost universally in Scotland, others only by people who speak broader forms of Scots rather than "Scottish English", and others are restricted to one part of the country. It is highly unlikely that any one person would use all the words in this book as part of their natural language. Where we believe that a term is regional, we have indicated this in the entry.

Dialects have been covered according to the number of speakers they have: roughly a quarter of the population of Scotland lives within twenty miles of central Glasgow, and the language of urban West Central Scotland is therefore dealt with in more depth than the language of Caithness or the Borders. (West Central Scots is also the dialect most often heard on television, whether in comedies or in detective series). This is not to say that one dialect is better Scots than another, simply that some are more widely spoken than others.

Official and technical terms. Scotland has its own distinctive systems of law, religion, education and local government, and each of these systems has its own terminology. Many of these terms are included. Also included are words to do with specific Scottish activities such as whisky-making, shinty, and piping.

Literary Scots. Different writers have used Scots in different ways. Some have written in what is more or less standard literary English, with a sprinkling of Scots words and idioms. Others have chosen to write using a language based on the speech of one particular area, be it Glasgow, Edinburgh or the rural Northeast. Yet others have attempted to create a modern literary Scots by using words from all parts of the country and, where necessary, going back to the language of Scots writers of the past for vocabulary. The objection often raised to this approach is that the result is far removed from the natural speech of any person from any part of the country. This split between literary and colloquial language is not unique to Scots – as the Scots language poet Sydney Goodsir Smith pointed out, "wha the deil spoke like King Lear?" – but because the standard written language of Scotland for the past three centuries has been English, the difference is particularly noticeable in Scots. For reasons of space only the most basic literary Scots has been included.

The History of Scots

When the Angles, Jutes and Saxons began to settle in Britain from the fourth century on, they brought with them their own Germanic dialects, and these became Old English, the language of the parts of England and Southern Scotland under Anglo-Saxon rule. This eventually developed into what is known as Middle English. Over the centuries, as the Scottish and English states emerged as unitary wholes, and followed their own historical paths, a language based on the Northumbrian dialect of Middle English (that spoken North of the Humber) emerged as one of the standard languages of Scotland. It is ultimately from this that modern Scots is descended.

Scots has always tended to define itself in terms of what it isn't: this early Anglo-Saxon derived tongue, initially only spoken in Southeast Scotland, was known as *Inglis*, to distinguish it from the Gaelic spoken in the

Highlands and parts of Southwest Scotland, the Welsh-related language of much of West Central Scotland, the Pictish of the Northeast, and the Norse of the Islands and the Far North. Only later, when it had emerged as the chief administrative and spoken language of Scotland (although Gaelic remained in widespread use), did it became known as *Scots* to distinguish it from the separate but closely related tongue of England.

Over the years, Scots has been much influenced by the English of England. Indeed, there has never really been a complete split: many Northern English dialects have descended from the same Northumbrian roots as Scots, with words such as *bairn* (a child or baby), *fell* (a mountain or hill) and *flit* (to move house) being found in Scots and Northern English alike. The main literary and political language of England (so-called Standard English), however, was one based on the East Midlands dialect spoken in London.

For many centuries, Scots and English developed in parallel: but the decision of the Church of Scotland to adopt a version of the Bible in English rather than in Scots following the Reformation, and the Union first of the Scottish and English crowns and later of the Scottish and English parliaments, meant that Scots came to have less and less social status. Many members of the Scottish nobility and middle-classes, eager to prove themselves good North Britons, made strenuous efforts to avoid all Scottish idioms and pronunciations.

But despite these attempts, Scots has remained in constant use, if mainly as a spoken language. The language of modern Scotland remains distinct from that of England, with its own words, idioms and grammar. A typical recent edition of one of the Scottish national newspapers, for instance, mentions a *depute fiscal* at a *Sheriff Court*, a wasp's *bike*, and a Church of Scotland clergyman who had *demitted* his post as a *minister*; Scottish greengrocers sell *syboes*; and in Scotland's pubs, drinkers continue to get *guttered* on pints of heavy and *wee goldies*.

It should also be noted that the trade between Scots and English has not all been one way: such commonplace English words as *cuddle*, *eerie*, and *greed* were originally Scots

The Dialects of Scots

Most authorities divide Scots into four groups of dialects, the larger of which have major subdivisions. There are many more subtle changes of dialect than can be covered here, and, particularly in areas where the majority of the population have lived locally all their lives, many people can distinguish between the speech of people from one town or village and their neighbours from a nearby area.

Central Scots, despite its name, is spoken throughout the area south and west of the Tay, with the exception of a small area in the Borders and East Dumfriesshire. It is the most widely spoken form of Scots, and can be divided into East Central Scots, West Central Scots, and Southwestern Scots. One of the chief differences between them is that the vowel sound in words such as *a'*, *cauld* and *wa* (all, cold, and wall) is pronounced *aw* in the West and *ah* elsewhere. Throughout the Central Scots area, the *-u-* or *-ui-* or *-oo-* vowel in words such as *guid* (good), *school* or *moon* is usually pronounced *-i-* (as in English *bid*).

Northern Scots is the other main form of Scots, within which Northeastern Scots, spoken in the area north of Stonehaven and East of Inverness, forms a distinct dialect. The most immediately obvious feature of Northern Scots is that *wh-* at the beginning of a word is usually pronounced *f-*, for instance in *fit* (what) or *fite* (white). The vowel in *guid*, *school* and *moon* is generally pronounced with an *-ee-* (as in English *heed*), but in the Northeast when this sound follows a hard *g* or *k* it is pronounced *-wee-* (*gweed*, *skweel*). All forms of Northern Scots frequently drop the initial *th-* in words such as *the*, *this*, and *that*. A noticeable grammatical feature of Northern dialects is the tendency to use *this* and *that* instead of *these* and *those* when referring to more than one person or thing: *did you see that two mannies?*

Island Scots. Orkney and Shetland formerly spoke a Scandinavian language known as Norn which had been superseded by Scots by the end of the 18th century. However many Norn words, such as *voe* (a narrow bay) have survived into the present day dialects. Other distinctive features of Orkney and Shetland dialects are the preservation of the distinction between the formal _you_ and the informal _thou_, and the pronunciation of _th_ as **d** or **t**, as in _tink_ (think), _blide_ (blithe, happy) or _da_ (the).

Southern Scots is spoken in Eastern Dumfriesshire and along most of the Border. Its speakers tend to say _-ow_ and _-ey_ at the ends of words, where people from elsewhere in Scotland would say _-oo_ and _-ee_ . It is sometimes referred to as the "yow and mey" dialect as a result.

The Highlands and the Western Isles, where Gaelic was (and some times still is) the main language, are generally described as speaking Highland English rather than Scots, although many Scottish words are in common use there.

The Vocabulary of Scots

The different histories of Scotland and England have meant that Scots and English have not only emerged from different Germanic dialects, but have absorbed words from different sources.

Much of Northern and Eastern Scotland was settled by the Vikings, and their Old Norse tongue has contributed terms such as _kirk_ (church), _brig_ (bridge) and _lowp_ (leap), some of which also exist in Northern English.

Later, political and trading alliances with France provided words like _ashet_ (a type of plate), _fash_ (to bother or annoy), and _gigot_ (a cut of meat).

Other trade links with the Netherlands endowed Scots,

particularly its Eastern dialects, with a number of words, with *howff* (a pub), *loon* (a boy or young man) and *pinkie* (the little finger) all coming from Dutch or Flemish.

Gaelic was formerly much more widely spoken than it is today, and many words have passed from it into Scots. Some words, such as *glen* (a narrow valley), *keelie* (a generally derogatory term for an urban working-class man) and *partan* (a crab), are general Scots, others, such as *bourach* (a heap or a mess), *cailleach* (an old woman), and *laroch* (a ruin) are restricted to areas in the North or West where Gaelic was historically strongest or where there has been large-scale immigration from Gaelic-speaking areas.

Scots also shares a number of words, such as *hooley* (a wild party), with Irish English: over the centuries there has been a long tradition of migration between the two countries, to the extent that dialectologists regard the language of some parts of Northeastern Ireland as "Ulster Scots" rather than a dialect of Irish English.

Lastly, there are a number of words that have come into Scots, and particularly its Eastern and Northern dialects, from the language of the travelling people, for example *barrie* (excellent) and *gadgie* (a man or youth).

USING THIS BOOK

Headwords are shown in bold.

Variant Spellings. Modern Scots is more often spoken than written, and many words therefore have variant spellings based on the writer's attempt to represent his or her pronunciation of the word. The main entry for a word can be found at the spelling which we believe is most common in current use. We have tried to minimise the number of variants shown to make the text easier to follow, but where a number of spellings are in common use, the most common variant (or variants) is shown after the headword. eg

cock-a-leekie or **cockieleekie** Cock-a-leekie is a soup made from a fowl boiled with leeks. Some recipes include prunes

fae (pronounced *fay*) or **frae** (pronounced *fray*) Fae means from: *some guy fae Tollcross; where'd he get that fae?*

The variant form is given an entry of its own, referring the reader to the main entry, unless the variant would come within five entries of the headword. Hence, there is an entry for **frae** but not one for **cockieleekie**

frae (pronounced *fray*) Another word for **fae**

Pronunciations are given for words which might be difficult or confusing for the non-Scots speaker. They are shown either by respelling, with the stressed syllable in bold, or by rhyming them with a word with a similar pronunciation.

ca' or **caa** (pronounced *caw*)...

caber (rhymes with *labour*)...

ceilidh (pronounced *kale-ee*)...

There are a number of regional variations in pronunciation in Scotland: in general the form shown is a West Central Scotland one, that being the most widely spoken dialect, but where a word is most common in a particular area, the pronunciation appropriate to that region is given.

Where more than one way of pronouncing a word is in widespread use, all these pronunciations are shown.

dicht (pronounced *diCHt* or *dite*)...

In respellings, each syllable has been shown in a form likely to be clear to all speakers of British English. However, the following points should be noted:

g always represents the hard "g" in *gun*, never the soft "g" in *gin*

ch represents the "ch" in *cheese* or *church*

CH represents the guttural sound represented by the "ch" in the Scots *loch* and in the German composer *Bach*

th represents the unvoiced "th" in *thin*, *three*, or *bath*

TH represents the voiced "th" in *this*, *father*, or *bathe*

iy represents a vowel sound used in Scots but not in English. It is the vowel in the normal Scottish pronunciation of *bite*, pronounced a bit like "eye" but shorter. It is used in the Scots pronunciation of *Fife* and *tide*, as distinct from the longer vowel in *Five* and *tied*

wh: words which, in southern English, start "wh-" but are pronounced as if they started "w-" (eg *what, white*) are always pronounced with an initial "wh" sound in Scots. This sound is rather like the "h" in *bit* and the "w" in *wit* pronounced almost simultaneously.

a', **aa** or **aw** (pronounced *aw*) A' means all: *It's a' the same tae me.*

Aberdeen Angus Aberdeen Angus is a breed of black hornless beef cattle originally bred in Aberdeenshire and Angus.

Aberdeenshire (pronounced *ab-er-dean-sher* or *ab-er-dean-shire*) **Aberdeenshire** is a former county in Northeast Scotland. It is now the name of a single-tier local council encompassing the old county plus Kincardine and most of Banff.

Aberdonian An **Aberdonian** is a person from Aberdeen. The dialect of Scots spoken in Aberdeen is also called **Aberdonian.** Something which is **Aberdonian** comes from, or is typical of, Aberdeen.

ablow (pronounced *a-blow*) **Ablow** means below: *in ablow the sink.*

aboot (pronounced *a-boot*) **Aboot** means about: *That's aa you incomers go on aboot.*

abune (pronounced *a-bin*) or **abeen** (pronounced *a-been*) **Abune** means above.

academy In Scotland, some secondary schools are known as **academies**. Originally, an **academy** was a public or private school in a **burgh**: *Bathgate Academy*; *St Margaret's Academy*.

ach (pronounced *aCH*) **Ach** is an expression of surprise, disgust, or resignation: *Ach, you don't really notice the smell after a while.*

act it To **act it** is to behave in a misleadingly innocent way: *He's acting it if he says he didn't know.*

Adam An **Adam** house, interior, piece of furniture, etc, is one designed by the architect and decorator **Robert Adam** (1728-92): *a grand Adam mansion in Charlotte Street.* **Adam** successfully emulated the harmony and grace of classical and Italian Renaissance architecture in the many British country houses he and his brother James (1732-94) built. His greatest Neo-Classical work is undoubtedly Charlotte Square (1791) in Edinburgh. The exterior of Culzean Castle in Ayrshire is a good example of his work in the Gothic Revival style.

advocate An **advocate** is a lawyer who has passed certain extra exams and is permitted to plead in the High Court. The English equivalent is a barrister.

Advocate Depute An **Advocate Depute** is a law officer who prosecutes in important cases on behalf of the **Lord Advocate**. The English equivalent is a public prosecutor: *The Advocate Depute asked him if he was aware of the possible consequences of telling lies on oath.*

ae rhymes with (pronounced *bay*) **Ae** means one or a single: *ae fond kiss.*

aff ① **Aff** means off: *Get aff the grass!* ② **Aff** also means from: *I got it aff ma sister.*

afore (pronounced *a-fore*) **Afore** means before: *I'll get home afore you.* **Afore** also means in front of.

after If someone says they are **just after** doing something, they mean that they have just finished doing it: *Wipe your feet. I'm just after cleaning the floor.*

agent An **agent** is a solicitor acting on a person's behalf, especially in a court hearing: *the defence agent.*

ages Someone who is **ages with** someone else is the same age as that person: *My James is ages wi her David.*

agley (pronounced *a-glay* or *a-gliy*) or **aglee** (pronounced *a-glee*) **Agley** means squint or askew. If something **goes agley** it doesn't happen or work out in the way that was intended or hoped for: *Their schemes had gone irreparably agley.* The word comes from the earlier *gley* squint, which comes from Middle English.

Ah Ah is a Scots word meaning I: *Ah said Ah hadnae seen him.*

ahint (pronounced *a-hint*) or **ahent** (pronounced *a-hent*) **Ahint** means behind or at the back: *Hing yer coat up ahint the door.*

aiblins (pronounced *abe-lins*) **Aiblins** is an old-fashioned or literary word meaning perhaps or possibly: *We'd had a few pints — aiblins a guid few.*

ain (rhymes with *rain*) **Ain** means own: *I'm going on my ain; He can wash his ain claes.*

aince (pronounced *eenss*) **Aince** is a Northeastern word meaning once.

airt An **airt** is a direction or point of the compass. From **a' the airts** means from all over the place.

Alba (pronounced *al-a-pah*) **Alba** is the Gaelic name for Scotland. A number of motorists in Scotland, even non-Gaelic speaking ones, have **Alba** on the nationality plates on their cars.

aliment In Scots Law, **aliment** is maintenance or support claimed by one person from another, especially money paid by one spouse to another when a couple is separated but not divorced.

Andrew, St St **Andrew** is the patron saint of Scotland. He was one of the twelve apostles of Jesus, and the brother of Peter. His feast day is on November 30th.

ane In some parts of Scotland **ane** means one: *A guid New Year tae ane and a'!*

anent (pronounced *a-nent*) **Anent** means about or considering: *a few remarks anent the meeting.*

Angus (pronounced *ang-giss*) **Angus** is a former county in the northeast of Central Scotland, the southern boundary of which is the Firth of Tay and the eastern the North Sea. It is now the name of a single-tier local council administering much the same area as the old county.

Arabs The supporters of Dundee United Football Club are nicknamed the **Arabs.** The origin of the nickname is unclear, but it may have started as a jocular reference to the one-time sandy condition of the Tannadice pitch.

Arbroath The **Declaration of Arbroath** was a letter sent by the Scots nobles to the Pope in 1320, asserting Scottish independence.

Arbroath smokie An **Arbroath smokie** is a small haddock that has been cured by being salted and then smoked unsplit over a fire. The name refers to *Arbroath*, a port in East Scotland in Angus, where this method of curing originated.

Argyll (pronounced *ar-guile*) **Argyll** is an area and former county of Western Scotland, consisting of the parts of the mainland west of the Firth of Clyde as far north as Glencoe, and the islands off this area. It is now administered by Argyll and Bute single-tier local council

Arranite An **Arranite** is a person from Arran, an Island off the Southwest coast of Scotland, in the Firth of Clyde.

arrestment In Scots law, **arrestment** is the seizure of someone's wages, bank account, social security payments etc, until a debt due to the person or organisation who started the legal action leading to the arrestment has been paid: *Arrestment of wages, claims the region, is the state-of-the-art method of collecting poll-tax arrears.*

as As is a word meaning than: *mair as yin.*

ashet (pronounced *ash-it*) An **ashet** is a large plate or shallow dish, usually oval in shape, used for cooking or serving food. The word comes from the French **assiette** meaning plate.

ask for To **ask for** someone is to make enquiries about their well-being or health: *Tell your Dad I was asking for him.*

Atholl Brose or **Athole Brose** Atholl **brose** is a drink or a pudding made from whisky, honey, oatmeal, and water. Double cream is sometimes added. The drink is named after an Earl of Atholl who, according to legend, incapacitated one of his enemies by spiking his well with whisky and honey.

at it To be **at it** means to be up to no good: *There is a general belief that all politicians are at it and not to be trusted.*

atween (pronounced *a-tween*) The word **atween** means between: *a sausage in atween two dauds o' breid.*

aucht (pronounced *awCHt*) or **echt** (pronounced *eCHt*) Aucht is a Scots word meaning eight.

aucht-day An **aucht-day** person or thing is an ordinary or unremarkable one: a Northeastern term: *jist an aucht-day kinna body.* The word comes from the earlier Scots way of referring to a week as *aucht days* (counting inclusively from Sunday to Sunday and so on).

auld (rhymes with *bald*) Auld means old.

Auld Alliance The **Auld Alliance** refers to the historical links between Scotland and France. These links started in the 14th century when both nations were the subject of English ambition and endured until the Reformation ranged the two countries on different sides of the Protestant-Catholic divide. During this period France had a detectable influence on the development of Scottish institutions and law as well as customs and manners.

Auld Enemy In Scotland, the English are sometimes referred to as the **Auld Enemy**, especially now in a sporting context: *The worst Scots nightmare, a gubbing by the Auld Enemy, was realised.* This phrase refers to the long history of conflict between the two countries.

Auld Reekie Auld Reekie is a nickname for Edinburgh. The name means literally *Old Smoky*.

ava (pronounced *a-vaw*) Ava is a word meaning at all: *It's no for the common fowk ava.*

avizandum (pronounced *av-viz-zan-dum*) **Avizandum** is the legal term for a judge's or court's private consideration of a case before giving judgment. A judge or court **makes avizandum** when time is needed to consider an argument or submission. The word comes from the Medieval Latin *avizare* to consider.

aw Same as a'.

awa (pronounced *a-waw*) **Awa** means away.

away To be **away** to a place means to go there: *I'm away to my work.* **Away!** is used to indicate disbelief or surprise. **Away wi ye!** is used to indicate contempt for a person or dismissal of what they have said. Someone who is **away wi it** is very drunk. **Away and...** is used in many expressions of dismissal: *Away and chase yourself!*; *Away and bile yer heid!*

awfy (pronounced *aw-fi*) or **awfu** (pronounced *aw-fa*) **Awfy** means awful: *Ah feel awfy*. **Awfy** also means very: *He's awfy untidy*.

aye or **ay** ① (pronounced *eye*) **Aye** means yes: *Aye, I'll be there*. ② (pronounced *iy*) **Aye** means always or constantly: *He's aye complaining*.

ayeways (pronounced *iy-ways*) **Ayeways** means always: *He's ayeways got a few cans put by*; *Ye can ayeways try again later*.

Ayrshire (pronounced *air-sher* or *air-shire*) **Ayrshire** is a former county in Southwest Scotland, on the east coast of the Firth of Clyde. It is now administered by three single-tier local councils: North, South, and East Ayrshire.

ba or **baw** (pronounced *baw*) A **ba** is a ball.

babby A **babby** is a slightly old-fashioned word for a baby.

bachle (pronounced *baCH-l*) A variant of **bauchle**.

back court or **back green** The **back court** of a tenement building is the shared paved or grassy area behind it.

backie ① In Dundee, Aberdeen and elsewhere in the Northeast, a **backie** is the back court of a block of flats: *All the young guys played football, on the backies and on the green.* ② A **backie** is also one of the many local terms for a piggy-back, which is also known as a **carry-code**, a **coalie-backie** or a **cuddy-back** in different parts of Scotland.

back of The **back of** an hour is the time just after it, up until about twenty past: *I'll meet you at the back of eight.*

baffie (pronounced *baf-fi*) **Baffies** are slippers.

baggie or **baggie minnie** A **baggie** is a minnow, especially a large one.

bagpipes The **bagpipes**, often called the **pipes** for short, are a musical instrument consisting of a set of pipes through which air is blown from a bag held under the player's arm. An individual instrument is known as a **set of bagpipes**. The type most commonly seen in Scotland, the **Highland bagpipes**, has one pipe with holes in it, known as a **chanter**, which is used to play the melody, and three pipes tuned to a fixed note, which are known as **drones**. The bag is filled by the player blowing into it. There also exists a smaller instrument, the **Lowland bagpipes**, which is sweeter toned and has the bag filled by a bellows which the player squeezes between his or her arm and side. The small Irish **uillean pipes** are also encountered, mainly among folk musicians.

bahookie (pronounced *ba-book-ee*) A Glasgow variant of **behouchie**.

bailie or **baillie** (pronounced *bay-li*) Bailie is an honorary title given to senior local councillors in some areas. It now has no legal significance, although formerly bailies had some of the powers of a magistrate The word comes from the Old French *baillif* a bailiff.

bairn In much of Scotland, a baby or young child is known as a **bairn**. In West Central Scotland the term **wean** is used instead: *The wife's expecting a bairn; The bairns came home from the school.* A person from Falkirk is sometimes referred to as a Falkirk **Bairn**, and Falkirk football team is nicknamed **the Bairns.** This use of the word is an allusion to Falkirk's town motto, "Better meddle wi the deil than the bairns o Falkirk".

baith (rhymes with *faith*) Baith means both.

baldie Another spelling of **bauldie**.

balloon A **balloon** is a Glasgow term for someone who is full of hot air and whose opinions, although loudly and frequently expressed, are regarded as worthless: *A pompous balloon who drivelled on about "mission statements" and "human resources".*

ballop (rhymes with *gallop*) In some areas, such as Galloway, the fly on a pair of trousers is known as the **ballop**: *I suppose we'd better tell him his ballop's open.* In other areas it is known as the **spaiver**, or simply as the fly.

balmoral (pronounced *bahl-maw-rul*) A **balmoral** is a type of round brimless cap, the top of which projects beyond the side and has a bobble on it. It often has a checked band round the side, and is usually worn at a slant. It is named after *Balmoral* Castle, a private residence of the British royal family in Aberdeenshire.

bampot (pronounced *bam-pot*) A **bampot** is a colloquial term for a foolish, stupid or crazy person, as are **bam** and **bamstick**. These terms all probably come from *barm*, the froth on the top of a fermenting liquid, which is also the source of the English word *barmy* meaning crazy.

bandit In the Glasgow area, any thing, person, or event that causes pain or outrage may be referred to as a **bandit**, especially in exclamations such as *ya bandit!*

Banff Banff or Banffshire is a former county of

Northeast Scotland, consisting of part of the southern coast of the Moray Firth and the area inland from it. It is now administered by Aberdeenshire single-tier local council.

banjo (pronounced *ban-joe*) To **banjo** someone is a Glaswegian term meaning to hit them a single hard blow.

Bankie (pronounced *bank-ki*) A **Bankie** is a person from Clydebank. Clydebank football team is nicknamed **the Bankies**.

bannock (pronounced *ban-nok*) A **bannock** is a round flat unsweetened cake which is made from oats or barley and baked on a griddle. **Bannock** is also short for **Selkirk bannock**, a type of round fruit loaf originating in the Border town of Selkirk.

Bannockburn (pronounced *ban-nok-burn*) References to **Bannockburn** are generally to the battle which took place near Stirling in 1314, at which the Scottish army led by Robert the Bruce defeated an invading English army and secured Scotland's position as an independent nation until 1707. The present-day village of **Bannockburn** is situated a few miles further down the **Bannock Burn**.

barkit (pronounced *bark-it*) **Barkit** is a word used in the Northeast which means very dirty, used particularly of something which is encrusted with dried-on dirt.

barley "Barley" is a cry used, chiefly in the East of Scotland, to call for a period of truce or a temporary halt to a game among children at play, used, for instance, when someone is hurt or needs to tie their shoelaces. The word is probably derived from *parley*, a ceasefire for discussion. In Western Scotland the word **keys** is usually used instead.

barley bree See **bree**.

baronial (pronounced *ba-roe-ni-al*) The **baronial** style of architecture is one popular in the nineteenth century in which buildings are ornamented with pseudo-medieval features such as turrets and mock battlements: *The magnificent turreted Scottish baronial style of the exterior of the hotel.*

barra (pronounced *ba-ra*) A **barra** is a wheelbarrow. Something which is **right into one's barra** is ideal and exactly in line with one's interests or desires. To **fancy one's barra** is to have an unduly high opinion of oneself. In the Glasgow area a **wee barra** is an informal way of referring to any small person that the speaker likes, or at least does not dislike. The Glasgow flea market is known as **The Barras**.

barrie or **barry** (pronounced *bar-ri*) Something which is **barrie** is very good or very attractive: *Your hair looks really barrie like that; We'd a really barrie time.* The word, which is of Gypsy origin, is mainly used in Edinburgh and the Southeast.

bastartin (pronounced *bass-ter-tin*) or **bastardin** (pronounced *bass-ter-din*) **Bastartin** is a swear word used, like damned or bloody, to indicate dislike or annoyance: *Watch whit yir daein wi that bastartin hammer!*

bate (pronounced *bait*) **Bate** is a Scots form of beat or beaten: *We got bate wan - nil.*

bauchle (pronounced ***bawCH-l***) *or* **bachle** (pronounced ***baCH-l***) A **bauchle** was originally a shabby or worn-out shoe. Nowadays the word **bauchle** is usually used to describe an ungainly or shabby-looking person, especially a small one: *a wee bauchle.*

bauldie or **baldie** (pronounced *bawl-di*) Someone who is **bauldie** or **bauldie-heidit** is bald: *a wee bauldie guy.* A **bauldie** is a bald person. A **bauldie** is also a very short haircut: *You wouldn't notice I'd had my hair done even if I got a right bauldie, would you?*

bawbee (pronounced *baw-bee*) A **bawbee** was originally a silver coin worth six Scots pennies. Later, **bawbee** came to mean a halfpenny. Although the halfpenny no longer exists, the word **bawbee** is still used to mean any small amount of money, especially in phrases implying miserliness or shortage of money: *the current economic climate — otherwise known as a serious lack of bawbees.* The coin was probably named after Alexander Orrok of *Sillebawby*, who became master of the Scottish mint in 1538.

bawface A **bawface** is a round, chubby face, or a person with such a face.

bawheid (pronounced *baw-heed*) **Bawheid** basically means the same as **bawface**. However, it can also be used as a cheeky form of address for a person: *Hey, bawheid!*

beadle A **beadle**, also known as a **kirk officer** or **church officer**, is a paid official of the Church of

Scotland, whose job includes assisting a minister with administrative work and placing the Bible in the pulpit at the start of a service.

beamer A **beamer** is a red face caused by embarrassment or guilt, or something which is so embarrassing or bad that it causes such a blush. The word is mainly used in the Glasgow area.

bear A **bear** is a usually derogatory term for a wild and uncouth young man, particularly one who drinks a lot: *The bar closed long before the bears' drooth was assuaged.*

beast Among farmers, a **beast** is a calf, cow, bull, or bullock, irrespective of its age or sex.

The plural can be either **beasts** or **beas**.

beastie A **beastie** is any small animal, nowadays particularly an insect, spider, or similar creepy-crawly.

beauty Ya **beauty!** is an exclamation of delighted approval or agreement: *A holiday on Monday. Ya beauty!*

beds or **beddies** In some areas of Scotland, the game of hopscotch is known as **beds**. The pattern of squares chalked on the ground on which the game is played is known as a **bed**. See also **pauldies** and **peever**.

beel To **beel** is a Northeastern word which means to fester or turn septic.

beelin To be **beelin** is to be furiously angry. **Beelin** is less commonly used to mean very drunk. A **beelin** is a Northeastern name for a boil on the body. All these senses are derived from *beel* (see above).

beezer Something which is a **beezer** is an extreme example of its kind, usually one which is bigger or better than normal. In particular, a cold but dry and sunny winter day is often referred to as a **beezer**.

behouchie (pronounced *ba-hooCH-ee*) or **bahookie** (pronounced *ba-hook-ee*) The behouchie is an informal, usually jocular, name for the backside: *Sit on your behouchie, you!* It is probably a combination of *behind* and *hough*, the Scots word for a thigh.

bell The **Bells** is the name traditionally given to the moment at midnight on December 31st when church bells are rung to mark the beginning of the New Year: *We always used to go to the Cross for the Bells, but it's got a bit rowdy these days.* When a group of people are drinking in a bar, the person whose turn it is to go and buy the next round of drinks is often said to be **on the bell**.

belong to To **belong to** a town or area is to live there: *I belong to Glasgow.* In Scotland, people sometimes say that the owner of an object **belongs to** that object, rather than the object belonging to the person: *Who belongs to this coat?*

belt The **belt**, also known as the **tawse**, was a leather strap with which schoolchildren were struck on the hand for punishment. Its use is now illegal: *I got six of the belt for fighting.* To **belt** a child was to punish them by hitting them on the hand with such a strap.

Beltane (pronounced *bell-tane*) **Beltane** is an old Celtic fire festival which originally took place on the first or third of May. It was also a former term-day, again on the first or third of May. In Peebles, **Beltane** is also the name given to the festivities accompanying the **Riding of the Marches**, which are held in late June. The word comes from the Gaelic *belltainn*.

beltie (pronounced *bell-ti*) A **beltie** is an informal name for the **belted Galloway**, a variety of **Galloway** cattle which is black at the front and rear but has a white band round its middle. They are most common in Galloway in the extreme Southwest of Scotland, where they were first bred.

ben ① A **ben** is a mountain. In this sense the word comes from Gaelic, where it is spelt *beinn*. **Ben** is often used as part of the name of a mountain, such as *Ben Nevis* or *Ben Lomond*. ② **Ben** also means in, within, or into the inner or main part of a house or other building: *Come ben the hoose: She was ben the kitchen making tea.* A **ben** is also the inner or main room of a house, especially that of the old-fashioned two-room cottage known as the **but-and-ben**.

Berwickshire (pronounced *berr-ick-sher* or *berr-ick-shire*) Berwickshire is a former county in the extreme Southeast of Scotland, on the North Sea coast and the border with England. It is now administered by Borders single-tier local council.

besom (pronounced *biz-zum*) Besom is a derogatory term for a woman or girl: *Cheeky wee besom!*

bevvy As in some other parts of Britain, in Scotland

any alchoholic drink is sometimes referred to as **bevvy**. A **bevvy** is a drinking session, and a particularly drunken one is sometimes called a **heavy bevvy**: *it's just another excuse for a good bevvy.* To **bevvy** is to drink alcohol, and hence someone who is drunk is sometimes said to be **bevvied**. The word is an informal shortening of *beverage*.

Bhoys (pronounced **boys**) Celtic football team and its supporters are sometimes referred to as **the Bhoys**. This is a mock Gaelic spelling of *Boys* which reflects the team's origin among Glasgow's Irish community.

bide To **bide** in a place is to live there: *They were biding in a flat near the harbour.* To **bide** in a state or condition is to remain in it: *We're no awa to bide awa.* To be able to **bide** a person or thing is to be able to endure or tolerate it. This sense is usually used in the negative, indicating that something is intolerable: *I cannae bide that man.* To **bide by** a decision is to comply with it, even if you disagree with it: *Party officials announced that they would bide by the outcome of the ballot.* The past tense can be either **bided**, **bid** or **bode**, and the past participle **bided** or **bade**.

bidie-in (pronounced *bide-ee-in*) Someone's **bidie-in** is the person who is living with them as their husband or wife although they are not formally married. The word is originally from the Aberdeen area, but is now heard elsewhere in Scotland, probably because it nicely describes a role for which there is no other informal term: *Katia Labeque, McLaughlin's bidie-in and sometime musical partner.*

bike A variant spelling of **byke**.

bile To **bile** is to boil. A fairly rude way of informing someone that they should go away, or that they are talking rubbish, is to tell them to **bile their heid**.

biling A **biling** of vegetables, especially potatoes, is enough of them to do for one meal; a Northeastern word. **Biling** also means very hot: *Can ye no open a windae? It's biling in here.* See also **boiling**.

billy A **billy** is an old-fashioned word for a man or lad, often implying that the person is a friend or workmate.

Billy or **Billy Boy** In the Glasgow area, a **Billy** is an informal name for a Protestant, as in the sectarian football chant which begins *Oh I'd rather be a Billy than a Tim.* The term is probably from the name of the Protestant King *William* the Third, who defeated the deposed Catholic King James the Second in the late 17th century.

bing A **bing** is a large hill-like mound of waste from a mine or quarry: *Large oil-shale bings disfigured the countryside.*

binger (pronounced *bing-er*) A **binger** is a West Central Scottish slang term for a losing bet, especially one on an unsuccessful racehorse.

birk A **birk** is a birch tree.

birl To **birl** is to spin or revolve: *She watched the clothes birling round in the washing machine.*

birse (pronounced *birss*) To **have** or **get one's birse up** is to be or become angry or annoyed. The phrase comes from an earlier sense of **birse** meaning bristle.

bit ① In parts of South and West Scotland, the place where someone lives is known as their **bit**: *Can Kirsty come out and play at my bit?* ② A **bit** is a boot.

black-affrontit (pronounced *black a-frunt-it*) or **black-affronted** To be **black-affrontit** is to be very embarrassed or offended by something.

black bun Despite its name, **black bun** is not actually a bun, but is a type of very rich dark fruitcake covered in pastry, which is traditionally eaten at New Year.

blackening A **blackening** is a type of pre-wedding ritual carried out in some areas where the bride or groom is smeared with mud, treacle or some similar dark-coloured substance and then often paraded through the streets by their friends.

black house A **black house** is a type of thatched house formerly found in the Hebrides and West Highlands, which was built mainly from turf and had an open fireplace in the middle of its one room The term is a translation of the Gaelic *tigh dubh*.

blackie A **blackie** is an informal name for a blackbird.

Black Isle The **Black Isle** is a peninsula in Northern Scotland, on the East coast slightly north of Inverness, which lies between the Moray and Cromarty Firths. It is probably so called because until the late 18th century much of it was uncultivated black peat moor.

blae (rhymes with *clay*) Something which is **blae** in colour is dark blue with hints of grey and purple.

blaeberry (pronounced *blay-ber-ree*) A **blaeberry** is an edible purplish-black berry of the type also known as a bilberry or whortleberry. It is also the name of the bush on which these berries grow, which grows wild on some moorland.

blaes (pronounced *blaze*) **Blaes** is crushed hardened clay or shale, reddish or bluish-grey in colour, which is used to form the top layer of a sports ground: *a blaes pitch*.

blate (rhymes with *plate*) **Blate** is an old-fashioned or literary word meaning very timid or diffident or, to put it in more informal terms, backwards at coming forwards: *She wasn't blate to tell him what she thought of him.*

blatherskate (pronounced *blaTH-er-skate*) or **blatherskite** (pronounced *blaTH-er-skite*) A **blatherskate** is someone who talks a lot, but rarely says anything sensible.

blaud (pronounced *blahd*) To **blaud** is a Northeastern word meaning to spoil or damage. Something which is **blaudit** is spoiled or damaged: *e tatties are aa blaudit; a park o blaudit neeps.*

bleezin or **bleezin fou** To be **bleezin** is to be very drunk. This word is in current use in the Northeast, but old-fashioned or literary elsewhere: *He wis fair bleezin.*

blether (pronounced *bleTH-er*) To **blether** is to talk or chatter. A **blether** means a conversation or chat: *It's nice to sit around and have a wee blether with friends.* An overly talkative person can also be called a **blether**: *He's nice, but* *a bit of a blether.* To describe something as **blethers** is to say that it is nonsense.

blin (rhymes with *pin*) **Blin** means blind. A **blin lump** is a boil or other swelling which never comes to a head.

blooter A **blooter** is a wild directionless kick of a ball. To **blooter** a ball is to kick it with more force than accuracy: *He blootered it over the bar.*

blootered A person who is **blootered** is very drunk: *He came home absolutely blootered.*

bluebell The **bluebell** is a plant with narrow leaves and pale blue bell-shaped flowers. It grows on dry grassland and moors, and flowers in the summer. In England it is known as the harebell. The Scots name for the woodland plant known in England as the bluebell is the **wild hyacinth**, although it is now often called the **bluebell** in Scotland as well.

Bluenose A **Bluenose** is a supporter of Rangers football team. The term is either derogatory or jocular depending on the speaker and tone.

boak or **boke** To **boak** is to vomit Something exceptionally unpleasant can be said to give you **the boak**, or even worse, **the dry boak**: *Even the look of liver gives me the dry boak, never mind the taste!* **Boak** is vomit: *There was boak all down the front of his shirt.* The word probably comes from the sound of someone retching or vomiting.

bocht (pronounced *bawCHt*) **Bocht** means bought.

bodhrán (pronounced *bow-rahn*) A **bodhrán** is a shallow one-sided drum, looking rather like a large tambourine, which is held in an upright position and played with a short two-headed stick. Originally Irish, it is now also used by Scottish folk musicians. The name comes from Irish Gaelic.

body (pronounced *bud-dee*) A **body** is a person: *a cheery wee body.* **A body** is a way of referring to oneself: *Can ye no leave a body alane?*

body swerve To **give something a body swerve**, or to **body-swerve** it, is to avoid it because you think it will be unpleasant or unenjoyable. It is sometimes shortened to **swerve**. The phrase comes from the image of a footballer dodging round an opponent.

boggin Something which is **boggin** is very dirty.

bogie or **bogey** (rhymes with *fogey*) ① A **bogie** is the name given in some areas to a child's homemade vehicle constructed from pram wheels, wooden boxes, etc. Elsewhere this is known as a **cairtie**, **geggie**, **hurlie** or **piler**. This sense is from the same root as the English *bogie*, a wheel unit on a railway carriage. ② The phrase **the game's a bogie** is used when something, originally but not always a children's game, has to be abandoned, because a situation has been reached where it is impossible to have a fair or valid outcome. This sense may be connected with *bogey*, an evil or mischievous spirit (as in *bogeyman*).

bogle (rhymes with *ogle*) A **bogle** is an old-fashioned name for a ghost. **Bogle** is also short for **tattie-bogle**, a scarecrow.

boiling A **boiling** is a hard sweet made from boiled sugar which has been flavoured and coloured.

boke Another way of spelling **boak**.

bonnet A less common variant of **bunnet**.

bonnie or **bonny** Someone or something which is **bonnie** is attractive and pleasant to look at: *I like your hair. It's bonnie; the bonnie, bonnie banks of Loch Lomond.* A **bonnie** amount is a large amount; now a rather old-fashioned use: *That must have cost a bonnie penny.* See also **bonny fechter** at **fechter**.

bonspiel (pronounced *bon-speel*) A **bonspiel** is a curling match. The origin of the term is uncertain, but it seems to be of Dutch or Flemish derivation: the second part is related to Dutch *spel* and German *Spiel* meaning game.

bool A **bool** is one of the large black balls used in the game of bowling, or among children, a marble. The games of bowling and marbles are both known as **bools**. If someone is described as speaking with **a bool in their mou** or **mooth** they are regarded as having an affectedly posh accent.

boorach or **bourach** (pronounced *boo-raCH*) A **boorach** is a word used in Northeastern Scotland to mean a group of assorted people or things. In the Highlands **boorach** has the slightly different meaning of a mess or a disorderly state or heap. Both senses are from the Gaelic *bùrach* a digging.

Borderer A **Borderer** is someone who lives in, or comes from, the area along the border between Scotland and England, in Scottish use particularly someone who lives on the Scottish side of the border.

Borders The Borders is the area of Southern Scotland near the border with England, extending from the Solway Firth just south of Gretna in the West to a few miles north of Berwick-upon-Tweed in the East. **Borders Region** is a former local government Region in the Southeastern corner of Scotland. It is now a single-tier local council and extends from the east coast to its border with Dumfries and Galloway, about twenty kilometres inland from the eastern end of the Solway Firth.

bosie (rhymes with *cosy*) **Bosie** is a Northeastern word meaning an embrace or cuddle: *Gie's a bosie*. The **bosie** is the bosom: *Stick that flooer in yer bosie*.

bothan (pronounced *both-an*) In the Western Isles, a **bothan** is a building where alcohol is illegally sold and drunk. The name comes from the Gaelic word for a hut.

bothy (rhymes with *frothy*) The word **bothy** has a variety of meanings, all of which ultimately have to do with it being a hut used for shelter. Historically, a **bothy** was a building on a farm providing eating and dormitory facilities for unmarried farm workers, most common in the Northeast. Nowadays, the term has come to mean a hut or cabin where workers, for instance those on a building site, can go to shelter from bad weather, for a tea break, or to eat. A **bothy** is also a sparsely furnished hut or cottage which hillwalkers or climbers can use for shelter or overnight accommodation. The plural is **bothies**.

bothy ballad A **bothy ballad** is a type of folk song which originated among farmworkers in Northeast Scotland. It usually deals with everyday rural life, often in a bawdy manner.

bottling A **bottling** is the Glasgow name for a pre-wedding ritual in which the bride-to-be is dressed up in outlandish clothes and paraded through the streets by her female friends and relatives to the accompaniment of banging potlids. Any man such a group stumbles across is expected to give them money in return for the privilege of kissing the bride. In some other parts of Scotland where this is carried out, for instance parts of Lanarkshire, it is known as a **creeling**.

bourach (pronounced *boor-aCH*) Same as **boorach**.

bowff or **bouff** (pronounced *bowf*) ① To **bowff** is to smell strongly and unpleasantly, like something which has decayed and gone off: *Eeugh! This beer's bowffin!* A **bowff** is a strong unpleasant smell. ② To **bowff** is also to bark, or to speak aggressively or cough in a way reminiscent of barking.

bowly or **bowlie** (rhymes with *jowly*) Someone who is **bowly** or **bowly-legged** has bow legs: *his rounded shoulders and bowly legs.*

box ① The **box** is an informal name for the accordion, often used in Scottish country dancing or folk

music circles: *He is a singer and a good box player.* ②
Someone's **box** is their head. This sense is usually
encountered in the idioms **out of one's box** meaning very
drunk, or **to do one's box in** meaning to baffle or
exhaust mentally.

boy A **boy** is an apprentice.

brae (pronounced *bray*) A **brae** is a hill or hillside In
place names such as *the Gleniffer Braes*, the word **braes**
means a hilly upland area.

braeheid (pronounced *bray-heed*) The **braeheid** or the
heid o the brae is the area at the top of a hill.

bramble In Scotland, **bramble** is a name for the
blackberry fruit and not just the blackberry bush. To go
brambling is to go out picking blackberries.

brammer A **brammer** is a West of Scotland slang
term for something very good: *Is that a new tie? It's a
brammer.* The word may be a Scottish form of the army
slang term *brahma* with the same meaning, and possibly
comes via the former British military presence in India
from *Brahma*, who is one of the most important Hindu
gods, and hence worthy of great respect and admiration.

brander A **brander** is the metal grating covering a
drain in the street.

braw Something which is **braw** is fine or excellent: *It's
a braw day.* The word is a Scots form of *brave*.

bree The liquid in which something edible has been
boiled or left to soak is known as **bree**. Some types of

soup are also traditionally called **bree**, such as *partan bree*, a type of crab soup. In the Northeast, to **bree** potatoes or other vegetables is to drain the water from them after they have been boiled. **Barley bree** is a poetic or old-fashioned name for whisky.

breeks Breeks are trousers or, occasionally, underpants. The word is a Scottish form of *breeches*.

breenge To **breenge** is to go somewhere or do something in a hasty and forceful, and usually clumsy or thoughtless, manner: *He breenged his way through the crowd.* A **breenge** is a forceful but clumsy rush.

breenger (pronounced *breenge-er*) A **breenger** is a West Central Scotland term for a person who acts impetuously and without proper thought.

breid (pronounced *breed*) Breid is the Scots word for bread. In parts of the Northeast it also means oatcakes.

bridie A bridie is a type of semi-circular pie or pasty consisting of pastry folded over a minced meat and onion filling. They originated in the town of Forfar in Northeast Scotland, and are therefore sometimes known as **Forfar bridies.** They were apparently originally served at weddings, hence the name, which is a shortening of *bride's pie.*

brig A **brig** is a bridge.

broch (rhymes with *loch*) A **broch** is a type of wide round stone tower, dating from the Iron Age, which was large enough to serve as a fortified home. The ruins of

brochs can still be seen in various places, mainly in the North and the Islands.

Brocher (pronounced *broCH-er*) A **Brocher** is someone from the towns of Fraserburgh or Burghead in Northeast Scotland. The name comes from an old sense of *broch*, a burgh or town, still used as local nicknames for Fraserburgh and Burghead.

brocht (pronounced *brawCHt*) **Brocht** means brought: *He's been weel brocht up.*

brock (rhymes with *lock*) or **bruck** (rhymes with *luck*) **Brock** is rubbish or broken or leftover pieces: *He called the plan "a load o bruck".* The word ultimately comes from the Old English *brecan* to break.

brogan (rhymes with *slogan*) Originally a **brogan** was a type of Highland shoe made from untanned hide and stitched with leather thongs, but nowadays it is used to refer to any type of heavy walking shoe, especially the brogue, a style of shoe decorated with a pattern of perforations along the seams. The word comes from the Gaelic *bròg* a shoe, plus the diminutive ending *-an*.

broo Same as **buroo**.

brook In the Northeast, soot is known as **brook**. Something which is **brookie** or **brookit** is sooty or dirty.

brose (rhymes with *rose*) **Brose** is an old-fashioned porridge-like dish consisting of oatmeal or peasemeal mixed with boiling water, a pinch of salt, and sometimes some butter. Compare **Atholl brose**.

bruck (rhymes with *luck*) The usual Orkney and Shetland form of **brock**.

bubble To **bubble** is to cry, snivel, or weep: *The wean came in from school bubblin.* A **bubble** is a cry: *She had a wee bubble at the end of the picture.*

bubbly Someone who is **bubbly** is in, or on the point of, tears, or is sulking: *Ah thought ye wantit to go. Well stick, bubbly!*

bubbly jock A **bubbly jock** is a male turkey. It is probably so called because of the noise it makes.

bucket In Scotland, a **bucket** can be a wastepaper bin or dustbin as well as a pail: *Chuck it in the bucket, will you?* A **bucket** is any undefined but large amount of alcohol. In this sense the word is usually encountered in phrases such as *we'd both had a fair bucket* or *he takes a good bucket.*

buckie A **buckie** is a whelk, a type of shellfish with a snail-like shell, some varieties of which are edible. The term comes from *buccinum*, the Latin name for a whelk.

Buddy A person from Paisley is sometimes referred to as a Paisley **Buddy**. St Mirren, Paisley's Scottish League football team, are nicknamed **the Buddies**. The word comes from the pronunciation of the Scots word *body*, a person.

Bully Wee The **Bully Wee** is the nickname of Clyde football team. The name comes from *bully*, an old-fashioned term meaning fine or admirable, plus *wee* reflecting the fact that Clyde were always one of the less powerful and successful of the Glasgow teams. (They now play in Cumbernauld).

bum To **bum** is to boast or brag. A boaster or conceited person can be spoken of contemptuously as a **bum**. These senses come from the earlier Scots sense, to make a humming or buzzing noise.

bumbaleerie (pronounced *bum-bah-leer-ree*) The **bumbaleerie** is an informal, often jocular, term for the backside.

bumfle A **bumfle** is a wrinkle, crease, or fold in something. If something is **bumfled** or **bumfled up**, it is untidily wrinkled or creased: *My skirt had got all bumfled up at the back.* The word comes from the earlier Scots *bumph* meaning a lump or bump.

bummer In informal speech, a **heid bummer** is someone who holds a position of power or authority in a place or organization: *None of the heid bummers around here have ever worked on the shop floor.*

bum up To **bum something up** is to claim that it is very good, or to make it out to be better than it really is: *Ach, it was okay, but it's no all it's bummed up to be.*

bunnet The word **bunnet** usually refers to a man's soft flat peaked cap. It can however be used of almost any flattish male headgear, such as a **tam o' shanter** or **balmoral**, and is sometimes also used of similar hats or caps worn by women.

bunnet hustler A **bunnet hustler** is someone, usually

middle-class or with a well-paid job, who deliberately puts on what they think is a working-class manner, or is excessively proud of their working-class origins; a derogatory Glaswegian term.

burgh (pronounced *burr-a*) A **burgh** is a town, specifically one which has been granted a charter by the monarch (a **Royal Burgh**) or by a noble (a **Burgh of Barony**) which formerly allowed the town certain legal privileges such as the right to hold a town fair and have its own town council: *A host of events are being staged in the town to mark the 400th anniversary of the granting of burgh status; the burgh surveyor.* The word is the Scottish form of *borough.*

burgh hall A **burgh hall** is the same as a town hall: *The meeting is to be held at the Burgh Halls in Linlithgow.*

burn A **burn** is the usual Scots word for a stream or brook. **Burn** is often used as part of the name of a stream: *the Swilcan Burn.*

Burns Night The 25th of January, the anniversary of the birth of the poet Robert Burns, is known as **Burns Night**, and a tradition has developed of celebrating his life and work on that date.

Burns Supper A **Burns Supper** is a meal held on or near **Burns Night** to celebrate the life and work of Robert Burns. It traditionally opens with a haggis ceremonially being brought into the room to the accompaniment of bagpipes. After someone has recited Burns' poem "Address to a Haggis", the haggis is eaten with turnips and mashed potatoes. After the meal, a speaker proposes a toast to "The Immortal Memory" of Robert Burns, before the evening continues with a variety of other toasts. The first Burns Supper was held in Edinburgh in 1815. They were originally men-only events.

buroo (pronounced *buh-roo* or *broo*) *or* **broo** The **buroo** is the dole, or the office at which people sign on for their dole money: *Has your buroo money come through yet?* The term comes from Employment *Bureau*, a former name for a Jobcentre. To be **on the buroo** is to be unemployed.

bursar In Scotland the word **bursar** can refer to a student who holds a **bursary** as well as to the chief finance officer in a university or college.

bursary A **bursary** is a scholarship or grant awarded to a student, either from a university or a local authority, usually as a result of financial hardship or obtaining one of the best marks in a special exam held by certain universities (a **bursary competition**). The word ultimately comes from the Latin *bursa* a purse.

burst The phrase **a hunger or a burst** indicates that the speaker thinks there is always too little or too much of something, but never the right amount: *We're either sitting twiddling our thumbs or rushing about trying to do three jobs at once; it's aye a hunger or a burst around here.*

but ① In the Glasgow area, **but** is often used as the last word of a sentence to emphasize what has been said in the rest of the sentence, especially when this contradicts or qualifies what has previously been said, either by the speaker or by someone else: *He's dead nice. Ah dinnae fancy him but; Ah'm no goin till Tuesday but.* ② A **but** is the kitchen or outer room of a house, especially of the two-roomed cottage known as a **but-and-ben**. ③ **But** is the past tense of bite.

but-and-ben (pronounced *but-and-ben*) A **but-and-ben** is a type of old-fashioned rural cottage consisting of two rooms, usually a kitchen and living room.

Bute (pronounced *byoot*) **Bute** is an island and former county in the West of Scotland, at the north end of the Firth of Clyde. It is now administered by Argyll and Bute single-tier local council.

buttery A **buttery** is a type of crumbly, butter-rich, bread roll originating in the Aberdeen area: *Two cups of coffee and a couple of butteries, please.* In the Northeast it is often called a **buttery rowie** or simply a **rowie**.

by In phrases such as **put by** or **lay by**, **by** means aside or away: *I'll put the rest by for you and you can collect it later.* **By** also means past: *The rolls are by their best but still eatable; Ach well, that's Christmas by for another year.*

bye A **bye** or a **bye kick** is a goal kick at football, taken when an attacker has kicked the ball out of play over the goal line. While it is in general use, most commentators and sports journalists prefer to use the more formal "goal kick": *Are you blind, ref? That was a bye, no a corner!* To **give something a bye** is to decide not to do it, or, if you are already doing it, to stop: *"We're gaun up the toon for a pint. Fancy comin?" "Naw, Ah'll gie it a bye the night"; That's a dreadful racket. Gie it a bye, will ye!* This sense comes from the sense of a team progressing automatically to the next round of a competition without having to play a game, either because it has been seeded or because there is an uneven number of competitors.

byke (pronounced *bike*) *or* **bike** A byke is a wasps' nest.

byre (rhymes with *wire*) A **byre** is a shed or stable where cows are kept.

ca' or **caa** (pronounced *caw*) Ca' means the same as call (in all its senses). Ca' also means to drive or propel: *to ca' nails into a wall*. To **ca' canny** means to be cautious or take care: *Ca' canny along this road*. To **ca' the feet frae** someone is to send them sprawling.

caber (rhymes with *labour*) A caber is a heavy section of trimmed tree trunk thrown in competition at **Highland Games**. The caber must be thrown so that it lands away from the thrower and on its heavy end. The sport of throwing cabers in competition is known as **tossing the caber**. The word comes from Gaelic *cabar* a pole.

caddis Caddis is a Northeastern word for fluff, especially the kind which accumulates under a bed.

cadger A cadger is a person who travels from place to place buying and selling goods, especially fish. A cadger is also a carrier of goods.

cadie (rhymes with *lady*) In Central Scotland a man's flat cap is sometimes referred to as a cadie.

cahoutchie or **cahoochy** (pronounced *ka-hootch-ee*) Cahoutchie is an old-fashioned word for rubber: *a* *cahoutchie ball.* The word is adapted from the French word for rubber *caoutchouc.*

cailleach (pronounced *kale-yaCH* or *kal-yaCH*) In North and West Scotland a **cailleach** is an old woman: *My memory of her is of a vague chain-smoking cailleach in eccentric garb and heavy henna.* The word is Gaelic.

cairt ① A **cairt** is a cart. ② A **cairt** is also a playing card.

cairtie (pronounced *care-tee*) A **cairtie** is the name given in some areas to a child's homemade vehicle constructed from pram wheels, wooden boxes, etc. Elsewhere this is known as a **bogie**, **geggie**, **hurlie** or **piler**.

Caithness (pronounced *caith-ness*) **Caithness** is a former county at the extreme Northeastern tip of the Scottish mainland. It is now administered by Highland single-tier local council.

Caledonia **Caledonia** is the poetic name for Scotland or the **Highlands**: *Caledonia, stern and wild.* Something which is **Caledonian** relates to Scotland or the Scots: *He failed to appreciate the nuances of Caledonian humour.* **Caledonia** was the Roman name for Northern Britain.

call In Scotland's Presbyterian churches, a **call** is an invitation to a clergyman by a congregation to become its minister: *The minister of Scalpay Free Church in Harris has accepted a call to Toronto Free Church.*

callant (pronounced *kal-ant*) or **callan** A **callant** is a young man or a lad. The word comes from the Dutch *kalant* customer, fellow.

caman (pronounced *kam-an*) In shinty, the **caman** is the long stick with a curved head with which the players hit the ball. The word is Gaelic.

camanachd (pronounced *kam-an-aCH*) **Camanachd** is the Gaelic name for **shinty** which is often used in connection with the sport. The **Camanachd Association** is the game's ruling body. The **Camanachd Cup** is the annual cup competition.

Campbeltown (pronounced *kam-bell-town*) A **Campbeltown** whisky is one produced around the town of Campbeltown at the southern end of Kintyre. The town was formerly one of the main Scottish distilling centres, although there are now only two working distilleries there.

camstairy (pronounced *kam-stair-ee*) or **camsteerie** (pronounced *kam-steer-ee*) **Camstairy** means quarrelsome, stubborn, or unruly.

canary To **have a canary** is to throw a tantrum or have an emotional outburst: *She'll have a canary when she sees this mess.*

Candlemas The 2nd of February, **Candlemas**, is one of the four quarter-days or term-days in Scotland.

canna (rhymes with *manna*) or **cannae** (rhymes with *granny*) In many parts of Scotland **canna** means cannot: *Ye canna park here; I cannae be bothered.*

canny Canny has a number of meanings the first of which, astute or cautious with money, is in general usage throughout Britain. **Canny** also means good or nice:

bonnie wee thing, canny wee thing. **Canny** can mean lucky or fortunate. In Scottish (and Northeast English) dialect **canny** means rather or quite: *I've been waiting a canny long while.*

cantrip or **cantraip** A **cantrip** is a spell or magic charm: *By some devilish cantrip slight, each in its cold hand held a light.* To **cast cantrips** is to perform magic spells: *A witch, that for sma' price, can cast her cantraips, and give me advice.* A **cantrip** is also a playful trick or a sleight of hand.

capercailzie or **capercaillie** (pronounced *cape-er-kale-yee* or *cap-er-kale-yee*) A **capercailzie** is a large European woodland grouse. In Scotland it is found mainly in the eastern Highlands from Tayside to Easter Ross, although it may be found as far west as the Loch Lomond islands. It has a black plumage and the male has a fan-shaped tail. The word comes from the Gaelic *capull coille* horse of the woods.

carnaptious (pronounced *car-nap-shuss*) **Carnaptious** is a word meaning grumpy, bad-tempered, or irritable: *He's a carnaptious auld devil!* The word comes from **knap** bite and the intensifier *car-*.

carry-code In some areas of Scotland, a **carry-code** is a ride on someone's back and shoulders Elsewhere this is known as a **backie**, **coal carry**, **coalie backie** or **cuddyback**.

carry-out or **cairry-oot** A person's **carry-out** is the takeaway drink or food they have bought from a bar, off-licence, or restaurant: *Let's get a carry-out before the bar* *closes.* A **carry-out** is also a restaurant from which takeaway food can be bought: *Does that Chinese carry-out sell cigarettes?*

carse (rhymes with *farce*) A **carse** is an area of low-lying fertile land near a river. The word is often used in place names such as *the Carse of Gowrie* and *the Carse of Stirling*.

cateran (pronounced *cat-er-an*) In the past a **cateran** was a bandit, robber, or mercenary of the Scottish Highlands. The word comes from the Gaelic *ceathairneach* plunderer, and dates from the 14th century.

caul In Southern Scotland a **caul** is a weir or a dam.

cauld Cauld means cold: *a wee dram to keep out the cauld; It was awfy cauld this mornin.*

cauldrife (pronounced *cawl-drif*) Someone who is **cauldrife** is prone to feeling the cold easily **Cauldrife** also means lifeless.

cauld-wind If **bagpipes** are described as **cauld-wind**, they are filled by bellows rather than by blowing.

causey A **causey** is a cobbled street, road, or way. A **causey stane** is a cobble or paving stone.

ceilidh (pronounced *kale-ee*) A **ceilidh** is an informal social gathering with folk music, singing, dancing, and storytelling. This kind of gathering, which is popular in the Highlands and Islands, is normally held in someone's house. In the rest of Scotland, a **ceilidh** is more of an organized evening of entertainment.

Ceilidhs take place in hotels or halls hired for the evening and involve Scottish country dancing to music played usually on accordions and fiddles. Some dances are for couples and some for larger groups. The word is Gaelic.

Celt ① (pronounced *kelt*) A **Celt** is a person from Scotland, Wales, Ireland, the Isle of Man, Cornwall, or Brittany, especially one who speaks a **Celtic** language. The **Celts** were an Indo-European people who in pre-Roman times inhabited Britain, Gaul, Spain, and other parts of West and Central Europe. Something which is **Celtic** is of or concerned with the **Celts** or their languages. **Celtic** is a branch of the Indo-European family of languages that includes **Gaelic**, Welsh, and Breton, still spoken in parts of Scotland, Ireland, Wales, and Brittany. Modern **Celtic** is divided into the Brythonic (southern) and the Goidelic (northern) groups. ② (pronounced *selt*) A **Celt** is player or supporter of Celtic, one of Scotland's largest and oldest football clubs.

Central Central Region is a former local government Region in central Scotland, which included the area on both sides of the River Forth and some of the southern fringes of the Highlands. It is now administered by three single-tier local councils: Falkirk, Clackmannan, and Stirling.

Ceol beag (pronounced *kyoll bayg*) Ceol beag is a class of music for Scottish bagpipes, consisting of marches, strathspeys, and **reels**. The phrase is Gaelic and means little music.

Ceol meadhonach (pronounced *kyoll me-on-aCH*) Ceol meadhonach is a class of music for Scottish bagpipes, consisting of folk songs, lullabies, and slow marches. The phrase is Gaelic and means middle music.

Ceol mor (pronounced *kyoll mor*) Ceol mor is a class of music for Scottish bagpipes, consisting of salutes, gatherings, **laments**, and commemorative tunes. The phrase is Gaelic and means big music.

ceud míle fáilte (pronounced *kee-ut mee-luh fah-ill-tya*) Ceud míle fáilte is a greeting often seen on place name signs for towns. The phrase is Gaelic and means a hundred thousand welcomes.

champit or **chappit** Champit vegetables are ones which have been mashed.

champit tatties or **chappit tatties** Champit tatties are mashed potatoes, one of the traditional accompaniments to **haggis** in a **Burns Supper**.

chanter A chanter is a pipe on a set of bagpipes that is provided with finger holes and on which the melody is played. The **chanter** can also be played on its own for practice. Compare **drone**.

chanty A chanty is a chamber pot.

chanty-wrastler (pronounced *chant-ee-rass-ler*) In the Glasgow area a chanty-wrastler is a contemptible person. The word **wrastler** comes from *wrastle* meaning to wrestle or struggle with something.

chap To **chap** on a door or a window is to knock on it: *I am directed to room five, and march up the stairs to chap nervously on the door.* A **chap** is such a knock: *Give the door another chap.*

chappit Same as **champit**.

chauve or **tyauve** (pronounced *chawv*) To **chauve** is to struggle, strive, or work hard, often with little to show for one's exertions. A **chauve** is a struggle: *It's a sair chauve for a half loaf.*

cheep To **cheep** is to whisper or speak softly. Birds also **cheep**, that is, chirp. The phrase **not a cheep** means not a word or not a sound and is often used in a command to keep quiet, such as *not a cheep out of you.*

cheeper A **cheeper** is a light kiss on the cheek.

chib In the West of Scotland a **chib** is an offensive weapon, such as a knife or a razor, used to stab or slash someone. To **chib** someone is to stab or slash them.

chief or **chieftain** The **chief** of a Scottish **clan** is its head or leader.

chiel (pronounced *cheel*) or **chield** A **chiel** is a lad or a young man. The word is in common use in parts of Northern Scotland, but is mainly old-fashioned or literary elsewhere. It is probably related to *child*.

Children's Hearing A **Children's Hearing** is the Scottish equivalent of an English juvenile court. They were introduced in 1971 with the objective of dealing with children under sixteen who are in criminal or family trouble. A **Children's Panel** of three trained volunteers makes an assessment of each child, based on evidence given by anyone with knowledge of the child, then recommends whatever action is needed to be taken. Recommendations are always made with the aim to help and reform rather than punish the child.

chitter To **chitter** is to shiver with cold.

chitterin' bite A **chitterin' bite** is a snack or sweet eaten immediately after a swim. It is supposed to prevent one from catching a cold.

chocolate In the Glasgow area the phrase **if he was chocolate he'd eat himself** is sometimes used of a person who is conceited or boasting about his achievements.

chuckie or **chuckie stane** A **chuckie** is a stone or pebble of throwable size: *throwing chuckies in the water.*

chuddie Chuddie is a name for chewing gum.

chum To **chum** a friend means to accompany them somewhere: *I'll chum you along to the bus stop.*

chunty heid In Northeast Scotland a **chunty heid** is a stupid person.

church officer or **kirk officer** Another name for a **beadle**.

Church of Scotland The **Church of Scotland** is the established church in Scotland. It has a **Presbyterian** structure, with each congregation being governed by an elected body of **elders**, and a Calvinist doctrine. The Church of Scotland has the largest membership of any church in Scotland, and the majority of Scots are members (active or otherwise). The secession of the Scottish Church from Rome took place in 1560 under the leadership of John Knox. In 1840, in what came to be known as the **Disruption**, a split took place among Scotland's Presbyterians and some members of the Church of Scotland left to form the **Free Church**. See also **Kirk**.

chute (pronounced *shoot*) A **chute** is a playground slide.

City Chambers In Glasgow, Edinburgh, and Dundee, the **City Chambers** is the seat of municipal government.

clabber or **glabber** In Southwest Scotland, **clabber** is a word for mud, earth, or clay. The word comes from the Gaelic *clàbar* meaning mud or a puddle.

clachan (pronounced *klaCH-an*) A **clachan** is a small village or hamlet. **Clachan**, being a Gaelic word, was first used of only Highland villages, but its use is now more widespread. The word is Gaelic and means stone.

clack or **claick** In Northeast Scotland **clack** is gossip or chat. To **clack** is to gossip or chat. This sense probably developed from one of its original meanings: the clattering sound a mill makes when in motion.

Clackmannanshire (pronounced *clack-man-an-sher* or *clack-man-an-shire*) **Clackmannanshire** is a former county in East Central Scotland at the Northwest end of the Firth of Forth. A single-tier council, Clackmannan, now administers much the same area as the old county.

claes (pronounced *klaze*) **Claes** are clothes. The saying **back to auld claes and porridge** means a return to normality after a period of jollity, celebration, or indulgence: *After Hogmanay it's back to auld claes and porridge for us.*

claik See **clack**.

claim In Glasgow, to **claim** someone is to announce one's intention to beat them up: *You're claimed after school.*

clan In Scotland a **clan** is a group of families with a common surname united under a single chief. Each clan member is, theoretically, descended from a single ancestor from whom the name of the clan derives. Members often bear the name of the founder preceded by **Mac**, a Gaelic term for `son of': *MacDonald* The clan system went into terminal decline in the years following the suppression of the 1745 Jacobite rebellion and the process was accelerated by the **Clearances** which forced large numbers of Highland Scots abroad to countries such as the USA, Canada, and Australia. Many of the descendants of these emigrants are proud of their Scottish ancestry and some occasionally return to Scotland for clan gatherings. The word is from the Gaelic *clann* family.

clanjamfrie (pronounced *clan-jam-free*) or **clamjamfrie** **Clanjamfrie** is a word used to refer disparagingly to a group of people, especially if one considers them a rabble. A **clanjamfrie** is also a varied assortment of things; a mixed bag: *The clamjamfrie of tenements, courtyards and closes which forms Edinburgh's Old Town.*

clap To **clap** an animal, especially a dog or a horse, is to give it an affectionate pat: *It likes ye to clap its wee head.* A **clap** is such an affectionate pat.

clappy-doo (pronounced *clap-pee-doo*) or **clabby-doo** A **clappy-doo** is a large black mussel. The word is from the Gaelic *clab* enormous mouth + *dubh* black.

clapshot Clapshot is a dish consisting of potatoes and turnips which have been boiled and then mashed together in roughly equal quantities: *Lunch is fillets of cod served with clapshot, roasted peppers and chilli oil.*

clarsach (pronounced *klar-saCH*) The **clarsach** was the ancient Celtic harp of Scotland and Ireland. Its use has been revived by folk musicians in both countries this century. The word is Gaelic and means harp.

clart or **clort** A **clart** is a lump of mud or something else unpleasant. A **clart** is also a dirty mess. The word is perhaps from the Middle English *biclarten* defile.

clarty, clatty or **clorty** Something that is **clarty** is messy or dirty: *The Tourist Board's inspectors are encouraged to give clarty accommodation the bum's rush.*

claw To **claw** something is to scratch it: *He winna claw an auld heid.*

claymore A **claymore** is a large two-edged broadsword used formerly by Scottish Highlanders. The later single-edged basket-hilted sword is often called a **claymore**. The word is from the Gaelic *claidheamh mòr* great sword.

Clearances or **Highland Clearances** The **Clearances** of the eighteenth and nineteenth centuries were the removal by landlords, often by force, of the inhabitants from some parts of the Scottish Highlands to make way for sheep and other more lucrative uses of the land. Many Highlanders were re-settled on poorer coastal land and encouraged to combine farming with fishing or kelp-gathering. Large numbers were driven off the land altogether and into emigration overseas or to the cities of the South.

cleek A cleek is a hook or any device shaped like a hook.

cleg or **clegg** A cleg is a horse-fly with a painful bite The word comes from the Old Norse *klegge*.

click If someone **gets a click**, they find themselves a member of the opposite sex with whom they may establish an amorous relationship.

clint In Southwest Scotland, a clint is a cliff or crag. The word is possibly from the Danish *klint* cliff.

clipe Another spelling of **clype**.

clipshears or **clipshear** A clipshears is an earwig The name comes from the resemblance of the pincers at the tip of the creature's abdomen to shears.

clishmaclaver (pronounced *klish-ma-clay-ver*) Clish-maclaver is a word meaning gossip or incessant chatter It is a combination of two Scots words, *clish* to repeat gossip, and *claver* to talk idly.

cloot Cloot is a Scots word for a piece of cloth or a cloth used as a duster, etc: *Dicht roon the sink wi a cloot.*

clootie dumpling (rhymes with *booty*) A **clootie dumpling** is a rich dark fruitcake served as a dessert, like a Christmas pudding. It is boiled or steamed in a **cloot** or cloth. Until the recent past, **clootie dumplings** were made as a birthday treat for children and, like Christmas puddings, were often made containing sixpences.

clort A variant of **clart**.

close (pronounced *klohss*) In much of Scotland a **close** is a narrow lane or passageway leading off a main street: *The restaurant is tucked away at the foot of a close off the High Street*. **Close** is often part of the name of such lanes: *Advocates Close*; *Mary King's Close*. A **close** may also be a passageway connecting a group of houses to a main street. In Glasgow and West Central Scotland the common entry and stairway from the street in a tenement building is known as a **close**: *Reared up a close in Govan, he feared no-one*. In Glasgow and West Central Scotland a **close** is also all the flats sharing such a common entry and stairway: *The whole close could hear the noise*.

cludgie In Scotland's Central Belt a **cludgie** is a toilet: *A wee boy's got locked in the cludgie*. The word is perhaps a conflation of *closet* and *ludge*, a Scots form of lodge.

Clyde The **Clyde** is a river in South Scotland, 170 kms (106 miles) long, rising in Southeast Strathclyde and flowing Northwest to the Firth of Clyde. It divides the City of Glasgow in two and was once the centre of the world's largest shipbuilding industry, where every type of ship from ocean liners and battleships to dredgers were built. At its peak 14 ships a day were launched on the Clyde, and the term **Clyde-built** was synonymous with quality.

Clydesdale A **Clydesdale** is a heavy, powerful workhorse of a breed that originated in Scotland.

Clydeside **Clydeside** is the area of industrial or post-industrial towns along the lower length of the river Clyde. **Clydeside** also refers to the shipbuilding industry in this area: *the Queen Mary, another famous Clydeside ocean liner.* **Red Clydeside** refers to the militant socialist trade union and political activity in the West of Scotland, particularly in the period between the two world wars. Unemployment and disenchantment with governments who were unable to deliver their promises of a better life for working people following the Great War led to greater militancy among the industrial working classes and this was reflected in the number of socialist candidates elected to Parliament from the area.

clype or **clipe** A **clype** is a person who tells tales or informs on his or her friends, colleagues, or schoolmates. To **clype** is to tell tales or inform on. The word is related to the Old English *cleopian* to call or name.

coalie backie or **coal carry** In some parts of Scotland a **coalie backie** is a ride on someone's back and shoulders; a piggy-back. The diminutives of coal and back are descriptive of the person being carried like a sack of coal. Elsewhere this is known as a **backie, carry-code** or **cuddy-back**.

coble rhymes with (pronounced *noble* A **coble** is a type of rowing boat. It has a flat bottom and is used on rivers and lakes, especially for salmon fishing The word is perhaps related to the Welsh *ceubal* a ferry boat.

cock-a-leekie or **cockie-leekie** Cock-a-leekie is soup made from a fowl boiled with leeks. Some recipes include prunes.

coggle To **coggle** is to wobble, rock, or be unsteady. Something that is **coggly** is shaky or unsteady.

College of Justice The **College of Justice** is the official name for the **Court of Session**, the supreme court of Scotland.

collieshangie (pronounced *call-ee-shang-gee*) A **collieshangie** is a loud and disorderly commotion or quarrel. The word is perhaps from *collie* the breed of dog and *shangie* a chain or leash connecting two dogs, as an obsolete sense of **collieshangie** is a dog fight.

collop A **collop** is a thin slice of meat fried in a pan. Fried minced beef is sometimes called **collops**.

common good The **common good** is the part of the property of a local authority, in the form of land or funds, that is at the disposal of the community. The **common good** can be used only on projects that advantage the whole community: *The finance is being supplied through the Perth Common Good Fund.* In this phrase *good* means goods.

Common Riding See **Riding**.

community council A **community council** is an independent voluntary local body set up to attend to local interests and organize community activities.

conceit To have a **good conceit of oneself** is to have a high opinion of one's own importance: *Journalists, in general, have a good conceit of themselves.*

connach (pronounced *con-naCH*) **Connach** is a Northeastern word meaning to spoil, in a variety of senses. To **connach** something is to waste or ruin it: *The crop was clean connached by the weather; He connacht the fairm wi his drinkin.* **Connach** can also mean to go off or cause to go off: *The thunder connacht the milk.* To **connach** a child is to spoil it: *It wis his mither at aye connacht him.* **Connach** also means to tire out: *The wee lad wis fair connached wi the lang walk.* The origin of the word is not entirely clear, but it may be connected to the old Gaelic *conach*, the name of a disease of cattle.

contermacious (pronounced *kon-ter-may-shus*) **Contermacious** is a word used, chiefly in the Northeast, to describe someone who is obstinate or intransigent. The word comes from the English *contumacious*.

continue In a Scottish court if the judge decides to **continue** a case, the proceedings are postponed or adjourned.

convener or **convenor** In Scotland, the chairperson of a local authority may have the title **convener**. The word is also used for the chairperson of certain committees, trade union branches, or political party branches: *the convener of the Kirk's board of communication*; *the vice-convener of Highland Regional Council.*

coo A **coo** is a cow. The plural forms are **coos** and the less common **kye**. Someone who is **at the coo's tail** or **at the coo's back** is late: *Come on Angus, we're going to be late again. You're aye at the coo's tail.*

cookie In Scotland, a **cookie** is a light round bun made with a yeast dough and not, as in the USA and Canada, a sweet biscuit: *a cream cookie.*

coom-ceiled A **coom-ceiled** room has a sloping or arched ceiling.

coorie or **courie** To **coorie** means to nestle or snuggle: *He cooried in to his mother's side.* To **coorie doon** means to cuddle up close: *Coorie doon ma bairnie.* The word is from the Scots *coor* meaning cower.

coorse (pronounced *koorss*) **Coorse** is a Scots form of coarse. Weather that is **coorse** is stormy or inclement. A **coorse** person is bad or wicked.

Corbett A **Corbett** is any of the 221 Scottish mountain peaks between 2500 and 3000 feet (approx 760 to 915 metres) in height. Compare **Munro** and **Donald**. They are named after J.R. *Corbett*, who listed them.

corbie (pronounced *korb-ee*) A **corbie** is a crow or a raven. The word is from the Old French *corbin* which came from the Latin *corvīnus* raven-like.

corbie steps See **craw steps**.

cornet The **cornet** of the **Riding of the Marches** in certain towns in Southeastern Scotland is the young man chosen to be the standard bearer of the procession. See **Riding**.

coronach (pronounced *kor-on-naCH*) A **coronach** is a funeral dirge or lamentation for the dead. The word is Gaelic and is related to the Irish *rānadh* a crying.

corrie A **corrie** is a bowl-shaped hollow on a hill or mountainside. The word comes from the Gaelic *coire* cauldron or kettle.

corrie-fisted Someone who is **corrie-fisted** is left-handed. A **corrie-fister** is a left-handed person. The phrase comes from the Gaelic *cearr* left or wrong hand.

COSLA (pronounced *koz-la*) **COSLA** is the acronym for the Convention of Scottish Local Authorities. As well as meeting to coordinate policies on matters of common concern, such as pay rates of local authority employees, it also allows representatives from each single-tier local council to express their collective opinions on national issues. COSLA regularly meets with, and makes recommendations to, **Scottish Office** ministers but it has no legislative or executive powers.

cottar or **cotter** Cottar is an old-fashioned word meaning a tenant occupying a cottage and a small acreage of land. A **cottar** is also a married farm labourer whose employer provides him with a cottage (a **cottar house**). The word is from *cot* a shortened form of cottage.

coup (pronounced *kowp*) or **cowp** ① A **coup** is a rubbish tip. It is also used to mean a dirty or untidy place: *Tidy up that coup of a room of yours.* ② To **coup** means to turn or fall over: *The wean couped her bowl onto the floor.* The word is from the Middle English *cowp* to strike.

coupon In Glasgow, a person's **coupon** is their face: *He's got a coupon like a Halloween mask.*

Court of Session The **Court of Session** is Scotland's supreme civil court. Established in the mid-16th century, it consists of an Inner House and an Outer House. The Outer House deals with first-instance cases while the Inner House deals with appeals. Although it is Scotland's supreme civil court, appeals to the House of Lords can be made against its decisions. Its official name is the **College of Justice**.

couthy or **couthie** (rhymes with *toothy*) Something that is **couthy** is plain, homely, or unsophisticated: *His poetry unaffectedly blended the couthy with the cosmopolitan.* A **couthy** room or home is comfortable and snug. A **couthy** person is sociable and friendly. The word is from the Old English *cūth* known.

Covenanter In Scottish history the **Covenanters** were Presbyterians who entered into bonds or **Covenants** in order to defend their religion against interference by state, Crown, or Established Church. The two most important of these Covenants were those of 1638 (the **National Covenant**) and 1643 (the **Solemn League and Covenant**). The **Covenanters'** Presbyterianism resulted in their persecution and many of them were killed fighting for their beliefs.

cowp A variant spelling of **coup**.

cow the cuddy Cow the cuddy is an expression meaning to outdo or be better than everything.

crabbit A person described as **crabbit** is grumpy or in a bad temper: *He's aye crabbit first thing in the morning.* The word is a Scots form of *crabbed*.

crack In Scotland, **crack** is gossip or a chat: *Come away in and give us your crack.*

craig A **craig** is a steep, rugged rock or peak. **Craig** is rarely heard on its own - crag is far more common - but is found in place names such as *Ailsa Craig* and *Craigforth*. The word is from the Gaelic for rock.

cran ① A cran is a crane: *a shipyard cran.* ② A **cran** is also a traditional measure of fresh, ungutted herrings. The measure was formerly a barrel, but was eventually set at the more exact 37.5 gallons (170.5 litres).

cranachan (pronounced *kran-aCH-an*) Cranachan is a traditional Scottish dessert made from whipped cream, honey, toasted oatmeal, and soft fruit such as raspberries. Whisky and **crowdie** should also be added, according to some recipes. The word is Gaelic and originally meant a drink of sweetened beaten milk.

crannie The **crannie** is the usual Northeastern name for the little finger. Elsewhere it is usually known as the **pinkie**.

cratur (pronounced *kray-ter*) ① In Scottish (and Irish) English **the cratur** is whisky: *Diners will have a chance to sample a drop of the cratur at the end of the meal; Italy is the third largest consumer of the cratur in the world.* ② A **cratur** is also a person: *She's a queer-looking wee cratur.* The word is a Scots form of creature.

craw ① A **craw** is a crow: *three craws, sitting on a wa'.* ② To **shoot the craw** is to leave, especially in a hurry.

craw steps or **corbie steps** In traditional Scottish architecture, **craw steps** are the small steps on the gable of a roof.

creel A **creel** is a large basket used to carry bread or fish. A **labster creel** is a wickerwork trap for catching lobsters and shellfish.

creeling A **creeling** is the name given in some parts of the country, such as the Motherwell area of Lanarkshire, to the pre-wedding custom in which the bride-to-be and her female friends and relatives parade through the town in outlandish dress, banging on pots and pans. Any man the group encounters is expected to give them money and in return is allowed to kiss the bride. Elsewhere, for instance in Glasgow, this is known as a **bottling**. The name was earlier applied to a variety of customs marking a wedding, some of which involved the carrying of a *creel*.

creepie A **creepie** is a low stool or a footstool.

creeshie Something that is **creeshie** is greasy or dirty. The word is from *creesh* fat or tallow.

cremmy A **cremmy** is a very informal word for a crematorium.

crivvens or **criffens** Crivvens is a mild exclamation of surprise. It may have originally been a shortened form of *Christ defend us*.

croft A **croft** is a small enclosed plot of land, adjoining a house, worked by the occupier and his family. **Crofting** in Scotland is restricted to the Highlands and Islands, where it originated during a period of agricultural improvement in the late 18th century. A **crofter** is an owner or tenant of a **croft**.

crowdie (rhymes with *rowdy*) Crowdie is a soft white cheese made by straining the whey from soured milk and beating up the remaining curd with salt. The word is perhaps from *crud*, an earlier form of *curd*.

crown agent In Scotland, a **crown agent** is a solicitor dealing with criminal prosecutions.

cruive (pronounced *kroov* or *kriv*) A **cruive** is a narrow space or enclosure, for instance a fenced-in run for hens. To **cruive** means to confine in, or as if in, a narrow space: *Hiv ye got the hens cruived in for the nicht?*; *Ye'll need tae cruive him in tae haud him on gaan til e pub.* The word, which is now most common in the Northeast, is related to the Gaelic *cró* a sheep-pen or hut, although this is probably derived from the Scots rather than vice-versa.

crummock A **crummock** is a shepherd's crook or a stick with a curved head. The word comes from the Gaelic *cromag* a hook.

crumpet In Scotland a **crumpet** is a large soft flat round yeast cake, about the size of an outstretched palm, full of holes on the top side. **Crumpets** are usually toasted, buttered, spread with jam or honey, then rolled up and eaten.

cry ① To **cry** means to name or call: *They cried me after my grandpa; What d'ye cry yon bird?* ② To **cry in on** someone means to pay them a visit: *I must remember to cry in on her next week.*

CSYS CSYS is short for Certificate of Sixth Year Studies. Although pupils in Scotland achieving good results in their **Highers** at the end of fifth year may enrol straightaway at a Scottish university, those wishing to stay on for another year at school may take **CSYS** subjects. These are roughly equivalent in standard to English 'A' levels, although they are studied for just one year. Compare **Higher**, **Standard Grade**.

cuddy or **cuddie** A **cuddy** is a donkey or a horse: *My legs are as stiff as an auld cuddy.* The word is possibly a nickname for *Cuthbert*.

cuddyback In Southwest Scotland, a **cuddyback** is a ride on someone's back and shoulders. In other parts of the country, this is known as a **backie**, **carry-code**, **coal carry** or **coalie backie**.

Cullen skink Cullen skink is a thick fish soup made from smoked haddock, potatoes, onions, and milk. The dish gets its name from *Cullen* a fishing village on the Moray Firth, and *skink* soup made from a shin of beef.

Culloden (pronounced *kul-lod-din*) The Battle of **Culloden**, which took place on April 16th 1746 near Inverness, was the final battle of the Jacobite Rising which began in 1745, at which the Government army comprehensively defeated the Jacobite rebels (who wished to restore the Stuart dynasty to the throne). Often incorrectly thought of as a battle between the Scots and the English, Culloden was in fact a battle in a British civil war which happened to be fought in Scotland. Many of the Government troops were Lowland Scots. The Jacobite forces were however predominantly Highlanders, and their defeat led to a concentrated attempt to destroy the traditional Highland way of life, with the powers of the chiefs being greatly reduced and tartan and the bagpipes being banned for a number of years. The battle is also known as the Battle of **Drummossie Moor**.

culpable homicide In Scots law, **culpable homicide** is the act of illegally killing another person without premeditation or malice. The English equivalent is manslaughter.

cundy In much of Scotland the gutter at the side of the road or the cover of a drain is referred to as a **cundy**. In Glasgow and West Central Scotland this is known as a **stank**. The word is a Scottish pronunciation of the English *conduit*.

cushie-doo (pronounced *koosh-ee-doo*), **cushat-doo** (pronounced *koosh-at-doo*) or **cushie** A **cushie doo** is a name for a wood pigeon. The word comes from the English *cushat* plus *doo*, a Scots word for pigeon.

cutty A **cutty** is a short, thickset girl. A **cutty** is also an old-fashioned word for an immoral or disobedient girl or young woman. **Cutty** also means short or cut short, as in **cutty sark** a short shirt.

cutty stool In former times people found guilty of immoral behaviour would be forced to sit on a **cutty stool** in Church while the Elders or other local worthies delivered a stern lecture and demanded the miscreant's repentance. The **cutty stool** itself was three-legged and very low, in contrast to the high-backed chairs from which the victim's accusers delivered their castigation.

dab To **let dab** is to allow something to be known: *She got him the tickets for his birthday and never let dab.*

dabbity (pronounced *dab-it-tee*) In parts of the West of Scotland a **dabbity** is a transfer picture moistened and applied to the back of a child's hand.

dachle (pronounced *daCH-l*) To **dachle** is a Northeastern word meaning to dawdle or loiter.

dad Another word for **daud**.

dae (pronounced *day*) To **dae** something is to do it: *Come on Fred, ye can dae it!*

daffin **Daffin** is playful or foolish behaviour.

daftie A **daftie** is a foolish or mentally deficient person: *Watch where ye're gaun, ye wee daftie!*

dale In the Glasgow area, a **dale** is a diving board, as found at a swimming pool. The word comes from a pronunciation of *deal*, the wood from which such boards were made.

dampt **Dampt** is a version of damned, used to give an appearance of not really swearing: *She went and lost the dampt thing.*

dander or **dauner** (pronounced *dawn-er*) A **dander** is
a stroll: *I'm just away for a wee dander.* To **dander** is to
stroll: *You can dander across the Solway sands to Rough Island, but
beware of being stranded by the incoming tide.*

danders In the Northeast, cinders, particularly those
from an old-fashioned smiddy fire, are sometimes called
danders.

darg A **darg** is a day's work or a task to be done. The
word was formed from a contraction of *day-work*.

Dark Blues Dundee football team is nicknamed **the
Dark Blues**. The name comes from the traditional
colour of the players' shirts.

daud (pronounced *dawd*) or **dad** A **daud** is a lump or
chunk of something: *a daud o' breid.*

dauner (pronounced *dawn-er*) Another word for
dander.

daur (pronounced *dawr*) To **daur** is to dare: *Wha daur
meddle wi' me?*

Dean of Faculty In Scotland, the **Dean of Faculty** is
the president of the **Faculty of Advocates**.

deasil (pronounced *deez-l* or *deesh-l*) To move **deasil** is
to move in the direction of the course of the sun or
clockwise. A **deasil** is a movement in this direction. The
opposite of this is **widdershins**. The word comes from
the Gaelic *deiseil*.

deave To **deave** someone is to deafen them or to
bewilder or weary them with noise or talk: *Grandad was
always deaving us with his war stories.*

dee To **dee** is to die.

deedle Another word for **diddle**.

deek In Edinburgh and the Southeast to **deek** something is to look at it or see it: *Deek this gadgie.* A **deek** is a look at something: *Have a deek out the window.* The word is from the Romany *dik* to look.

deem A **deem** is a Northeastern word for a woman: *She's an awfu deem.* A maid or female servant on a farm in the Northeast is also known as a **deem**. The word is a local form of *dame*.

defamation In Scots Law **defamation** is the utterance of material injurious to a person's reputation whether in published or spoken form. In English Law two separate terms are used: libel or slander.

defender In Scots Law the **defender** is the defendant in a civil law case.

deid (pronounced *deed*) To be **deid** is to be dead: *Ye cannae spend a dollar when you're deid; There is no way I could stay here, the place is deid.*

deif (pronounced *deef*) To be **deif** is to be deaf: *I'm talking to you! Are ye deif or something?*

deifie (rhymes with *leafy*) In the Glasgow area to **sling someone a deifie** is to disregard them or pretend that one has not heard what they have said.

deil (pronounced *deal*) The **deil** is the devil. The **deil's books** or **deil's picture books** means a set of playing cards.

delict (pronounced *dee-likt*) In Scots Law a **delict** is a wrongful act for which the person injured has the right to a civil remedy.

demit (pronounced *dee-mit*) To **demit** a job or position is a rather formal term meaning to resign from it: *He resigned from the presbytery, and demitted his status as a minister.* In formal language, resignation from a job or position is sometimes called **demission**. The word comes from the Latin *dīmittere* meaning to send forth, discharge or renounce.

den A **den** is a narrow wooded valley. The word is found as part of several place names: *Denholm; Cardenden.* In children's games such as tig a place where one is safe from being caught is called **den**.

depute (pronounced *depp-yoot*) In Scotland a deputy is known as a **depute**: *The committee convenor and her depute both supported the ban; the authority's Depute Director of Education.*

Diamonds Airdrie football team is nicknamed **the Diamonds**. This refers to their traditional strip, which has a white top with a red V on the front and back, the legs of the V joining at the shoulders to form a diamond shape.

dicht (pronounced *diCHt* or *dite*) To **dicht** something is to wipe it clean: *Dicht 'roon the sink.* A **dicht** is a wipe: *Gie your face a dicht.* The word comes from the Old English *dibt* to arrange.

diddle or **deedle** To **diddle** is to sing wordlessly or with meaningless words to imitate the sound of instrumental music. The word represents one of the vocal sounds used.

diddy A **diddy** is a female breast or nipple. In the Glasgow area a foolish person may also be called a **diddy**.

ding To **ding** something is to strike it. In Eastern Scotland heavy rain may be said to **ding doon**.

dinger (pronounced *ding-er*) In some parts of Scotland to **go one's dinger** means to lose one's temper or to do something enthusiastically: *Maxwell went his dinger about the launch that very day of Scotland's first Trident submarine.*

dinna or **dinnae** In many parts of Scotland **dinna** means do not: *I dinna ken the laddie's name; Dinnae upset yersel.*

dinner school In the Glasgow area a school canteen is often referred to as the **dinner school**: *I forgot my pieces, so I'll need to go to the dinner school.*

dirk A **dirk** is a kind of dagger formerly carried by Highlandmen. To **dirk** someone is to stab them with such a weapon.

dirl To **dirl** is to vibrate or shake. To **dirl** something is to make it vibrate or shake by striking it.

disnae (pronounced *diz-nee*) The word **disnae** means does not: *She disnae eat meat.*

Disruption The **Disruption** is the name given to the historic split in the Church of Scotland in 1843 when over a third of its ministers left to form the **Free Church of Scotland**. See **Free Church** (and also **Wee Free**).

District A **District** was one of the fifty three smaller units of local government which mainland Scotland was divided into between 1975 and 1996. Each District was part of a Region but had its own elected council which was solely responsible for housing, environmental health, and refuse collection. Both Districts and Regions have since been replaced by single-tier local councils of which there are twenty nine: *Cunninghame District.* **District** also means of or relating to one of these local authorities: *Monklands District Council; He went to see his local District councillor, who said that there was nothing she could do about the problem, as roads maintenance was a responsibility of the Region.* Compare **Islands Council** and **Region**.

dizzy In the Glasgow area to give someone a **dizzy** is to stand them up when on a date: *That's the last time he'll gie me a dizzy.*

dochter (pronounced *dawCH-ter*) A **dochter** is a daughter: *his dochter Janet.*

docken In Scotland the dock plant or any of its leaves is called a **docken**: *Rub that nettle-sting with a docken.* The word is also used to mean a thing of no value or importance: *It's no worth a docken.*

dog In the Glasgow area to **dog** something (especially school or a lesson) is to play truant from it: *What's this I hear about you doggin school?*

dominie (pronounced *dom-in-ee*) **Dominie** is a rather old-fashioned word for a schoolmaster: *I remember those awful mornings at school when the dominie went round the class for* *the mental arithmetic tests.* The word comes from the Latin *dominus* lord.

Donald A **Donald** is a term for any Scottish Lowland hill of 2000 feet (610 metres) or more. Compare **Munro** and **Corbett**. The term is named after Percy *Donald* who first made a list of them.

donnert (pronounced *don-nert*) Someone who is described as **donnert** is either stupid or stunned. The exact origin of the word is unclear, but it probably ultimately comes from the Middle English *donnen* or *dunnen* to make a din, with the sense developing via the idea of someone being stupefied by a loud noise.

Dons Aberdeen Football Club is nicknamed **the Dons**: *He was sent off when he elbowed the Dons skipper.* The name may have originated as a shortening of *Aberdonians.*

doo A **doo** was originally the Scots word for a dove, but is now also commonly used to mean a pigeon.

doocot or **dooket** (pronounced *dook-et*) The word **doocot** means a dovecote or a pigeon loft. It is also used to refer to a pigeonhole: *If I'm not about, leave a note for me in my doocot.*

dook or **douk** ① To **dook** is to duck, dip, or bathe. A **dook** is an act of ducking, dipping, or bathing: *Who's for a dook in the watter?* ② A **dook** can also be a wooden plug driven into a wall to hold a screw or nail. In this sense, the word is probably of Dutch or Low German origin: compare the Frisian *douk* meaning a spigot.

dookers In some parts of Scotland swimming trunks are known as **dookers**.

dookin **Dookin for apples** is a traditional Halloween game involving trying to pick floating apples out of a basin of water using only one's teeth.

doolie In some parts of Scotland a **doolie** is a foolish person: *Don't just stand there like a doolie!*

doon **Doon** is a Scots word meaning down: *I just put the packet doon for a meenit and when I looked again it was gone.*

doon-bye **Doon-bye** means down there, referring to a place already mentioned: *"Is it near Kirkcaldy he stays?" "Aye, he lives doon-bye."*

Doonhamer (pronounced *doon-hame-er*) A person from the town of Dumfries may be informally referred to as a **Doonhamer**. Dumfries's football team, Queen of the South, is nicknamed the **Doonhamers**. The word comes from the habit of Dumfries people referring to their home town as *doon hame* down (at) home.

doon the watter In the Glasgow area, to go **doon the watter** is to take a pleasure cruise along the Firth of Clyde. Glaswegians, when steam ships were common on the Clyde, would go **doon the watter** in their thousands to resorts such as Rothesay and Millport during the Glasgow Fair (see **Fair**).

doot A **doot** means a doubt: *I hae ma doots.* To **doot** something is to doubt it: *I doot I'll need tae gang hame an look after the dinner.*

Doric The **Doric** is a name applied to the Scots dialect of the Northeast of the country. Compare **Lallans**. The word was formerly used to describe any British rural dialect, especially one from the Scottish Lowlands, comparing them to the rustic form of Ancient Greek spoken by the *Dorians*.

dot To **dot** to a place is to go there on foot for a brief period, to pop or nip there. It is always used with a preposition such as *about, out* or *round*: *I'm just dotting out to the shops; I dotted round to see my mother.*

dottled Someone who is **dottled** is confused, muddled or senile: *I may be old, but I'm no dottled yet.* The word, which is mainly found in the Northeast, is related to the English *dotage*.

doubt In Scots usage to **doubt** something can mean to be inclined to believe it: *I doubt it's going to rain.*

douce (rhymes with *noose*) **Douce** means quiet, sober, or sedate: *Of all the douce suburbs of Edinburgh, none is more douce and worthy than Colinton.* The word comes from the French *douce* meaning sweet.

doughball In the Glasgow area a **doughball** means an idiot.

dough heid (pronounced *doe-heed*) In the Glasgow area to call someone a **dough heid** is to say they are stupid.

doup (pronounced *dowp*) A person's **doup** is their buttocks: *I'll skelp yer doup!* The word comes from the Dutch *dop* a shell.

dowt A **dowt** is a cigarette-end. The word comes from *dout* an English dialect word meaning to extinguish a fire.

dram The word **dram** is used to mean a drink of whisky rather than a precise measure of it: *You'll have time for a dram?*

drap A **drap** is a drop of something: *There's a wee drap tea in the pot.* To **drap** something is to drop it: *The wee girl's drapped her ice-lolly.*

drappie A **drappie** is a little drop, especially of spirits: *Then we had a drappie, just to make us happy.*

dree one's weird To **dree one's weird** means to endure one's fate.

dreep A **dreep** is a drip. To **dreep** is to drip. To **dreep** something (for example a wall) is to get down from it by lowering oneself with the hands as far as possible and then letting oneself drop the rest of the way.

dreich (pronounced *dreeCH*) To describe something as **dreich** is to say that it is dreary or tedious: *It's one of the dreichest stretches of road in all Scotland.* Wet, dismal weather or a period of this may also be described as **dreich**: *It's awful dreich this morning.*

drone The **drones** on a set of bagpipes are the three pipes which are each tuned to a fixed note. Compare **chanter**.

drookit or **droukit** (pronounced *drook-it*) When something or someone is **drookit** it or they are drenched or soaked.

drooth or **drouth** A **drooth** is a thirst: *You've got some drooth on ye the night!* The word is a Scots form of *drought*.

droothy or **drouthy** A thirsty person may be described as **droothy**, especially if it is alcoholic drink that is desired: *Scotland has more than 10 breweries producing real ales for the droothy cognoscenti.*

drum A **drum** is a narrow ridge or hill. The word often appears as part of place names, such as *Drumchapel* or *Drumnadrochit.* The word comes from the Gaelic *druim.*

dry-stane A construction built by fitting stones together without mortar may be described as **dry-stane**, especially a field wall (a **dry-stane dyke**).

dub A **dub** is a puddle or pool of muddy water. The word is from the Low German *dobbe.*

dug A **dug** is a dog: *Alsatians and sundry other dugs roam in packs through the scheme.*

Dumfries and Galloway (pronounced *dum-freess and gal-la-way*) **Dumfries and Galloway** is a former local government Region in the Southwestern corner of Scotland. It is now a single-tier local council and extends from the west coast to a border with Borders Council about twenty kilometres inland from the eastern end of the Solway Firth.

Dumfriesshire (pronounced *dum-freess-sher* or *dum-freess-shire*) **Dumfriesshire** is a former county in Southern Scotland. Its southern boundaries lie on the northeastern coast of the Solway Firth and the westernmost part of the border with England. It is now administered by Dumfries and Galloway single-tier local council.

dun A **dun** is a type of small iron age fort or fortified dwelling. **Dun** is found as part of many place names, such as *Dundee* and *Dunbar*. It is sometimes altered to **Dum**, as in *Dumbarton* and *Dumfries*. The word was originally Gaelic.

Dunbartonshire (pronounced *dun-**bart**-un-sher* or *dun-**bart**-un-shire*) **Dunbartonshire** is a former county of West Central Scotland, notable for being in two distinct parts, **East Dunbartonshire** and **West Dunbartonshire**, which were separated by parts of Stirlingshire and Lanarkshire. The county's name is spelled **Dunbartonshire** with an "n" although its county town is Dumbarton spelled with an "m". It is now administered by two single-tier local councils: East Dunbartonshire and Dumbarton & Clydebank.

Dundee cake **Dundee cake** is a rich fruit cake decorated with almonds.

Dundonian (pronounced *dun-**doe**-ni-an*) A **Dundonian** is a person from Dundee: *A Dundonian who knows her home town isn't the greatest place on earth but still has a soft spot for it.* Someone or something **Dundonian** is from or typical of Dundee: *The traditional Dundonian industries of jute, jam, and journalism.* **Dundonian** is also the name given to the dialect of Scots spoken in Dundee. It is essentially a form of East Central Scots, but shares some vocabulary with Northeastern Scots, the boundary between the two dialects running near the city. To many people, the most distinctive feature of the Dundonian accent is that the sound of "I" or "eye" is pronounced *eh*. For example, the statement "Aye, I'll try a pie" could be said to sound like *Eh, Eh'll treh a peh.*

dundy money In the Glasgow area **dundy money** is a slang term for a redundancy payment: *He blew his dundy money on a new motor.*

Dunlop cheese (pronounced *dun-lop*) **Dunlop** is a hard mature cheese, similar to cheddar, made from unskimmed milk. It is named after a village in Ayrshire.

dunny The cellar or basement of a tenement building is often known as the **dunny**: *It's awfy dark doon in the dunny.* The word is possibly a shortening of *dungeon.*

dunt A **dunt** is a blow or a thump: *a dunt in the ribs.* It can also mean the injury caused by such a blow. To **dunt** is to strike or hit: *He dunted his head on the luggage rack when he stood up.*

dux In some Scottish schools, especially formerly, the top pupil in a class or the whole school is called the **dux**. The word comes from the Latin word for leader.

dwam or **dwaum** A **dwam** is a stupor or a daydream, especially in the phrase **in a dwam**: *Sorry, I didn't catch what you said. I was away in a wee dwam.* To **dwam** is to faint or fall ill. The term is of Germanic origin: compare the Old English *dwolma* confusion and Old High German *twalm* giddiness.

dyke A **dyke** is a wall, especially one separating fields or around a garden: *In Caithness, the dykes are typically composed of massive slabs of local flagstone.* To **jump** or **lowp the dyke** is to change one's allegiance.

e or **ee** In broad Northern Scots **e** is often used instead of "the": *e quine*; *ee midgies*. The initial "th-" is also sometimes omitted in words such as "this", "that", "they" and "there": *work at needs done*; *ere isna aa that mony*.

eariewig (pronounced *ear-ee-wig*) **Eariewig** means earwig in all its senses.

easter The **easter** part of an area is the part of it which is furthest east. The word is generally used in place names such as *Easter Ross* or *Easter Howgate*.

East Lothian (pronounced *loathe-ee-an*) **East Lothian** is a former county of East Central Scotland, on the North Sea coast and the southeastern end of the Firth of Forth. It is now the name of a single-tier local council administering much the same area as the old county.

easy-oasy A person who is **easy-oasy** is very easy-going, laid-back, or slightly lazy: *We're far too easy-oasy in defence*.

echt (pronounced *eCHt*) or **aucht** (pronounced *awCHt*) The word **echt** means eight.

Edinburgh rock **Edinburgh rock** is a light, brittle, stick-shaped confection made of cream of tartar, water, sugar, colouring, and flavouring. It was first made in Edinburgh.

ee ① An **ee** is an eye. The plural form is **een**. ② A variant spelling of **e**.

eedle-doddle Someone described as an **eedle-doddle** is a rather carefree and nonchalant person, or a day-dreamer. The word is perhaps from *idle* and *dawdle*.

eejit In Scotland (and Ireland) an **eejit** is an idiot: *Beat it, ya big eejit ye!*; *There ought to be stronger measures taken to ban such eejits from being anywhere near guns.*

eeksie-peeksie Eeksie-peeksie is a phrase meaning absolutely equal or even: *Share them out between ye, eeksie-peeksie.*

een Een is the plural form of **ee**.

eese (rhymes with *peace*) Eese is a Northern form of use (the noun): *Fit eese is at?* The verb is generally "use".

efter Efter is a Scots form of after: *She's a guid wee wife, son. She'll look efter ye.*

eident (rhymes with *trident*) Eident is a literary or old-fashioned word meaning hard-working or diligent: *Be eident and civil to them baith.*

eightsome reel An **eightsome reel** is a lively Scottish country dance for four couples who combine in square and circular formations. See **reel**.

EIS EIS stands for the Educational Institute of Scotland. It is Scotland's largest teaching union.

elder In a Presbyterian Church an **elder** is an ordained church member with official duties. There are two types of **elder. Ruling elders** are involved in the government of their church as members of the **kirk session**, whilst **teaching elders** are members of the ministry and are therefore allowed to teach.

Episcopal Church The **Episcopal Church** is the autonomous Scottish branch of the Anglican Communion, and is therefore in full communion with (although independent of) the Church of England.

erse Erse is a Scottish form of arse: *Shift yer erse, wee man!*

Erse Erse is a rare and old-fashioned name for **Gaelic**: *The villagers conversed in Erse.* Something that is **Erse** relates to Gaelic and its speakers. The word comes from Lowland Scots *Erisch* Irish (Gaelic being regarded as of Irish origin).

ettle To **ettle** means to attempt to do something: *ettlin tae scrieve in Doric.* The word comes from the Old Norse *ætla* to conjecture.

export Export is a beer slightly stronger and darker than **heavy**. It is to be found on draught at most Scottish public houses, although, as its name suggests, it was originally brewed for consumers abroad.

fa (pronounced *faw*) To **fa** is to fall. A **fa** is a fall.

factor A **factor** is the manager of an estate. In tenement buildings in some parts of Scotland a **factor** is an agent to whom individual flat-owners pay a regular sum for maintaining the common parts of the building (such as the roof).

Faculty of Advocates The **Faculty of Advocates** is the professional association of **advocates** in Scotland.

fae (pronounced *fay*) or **frae** (pronounced *fray*) **Fae** means from: *some guy fae Tollcross; Where'd he get that fae?*

fail A **fail** is a turf or sod. The word is possibly from the Gaelic *fàl* a sod.

fair The word **fair** means very: *I'm fair sick of this.* **Fair** can also mean certainly: *She's fair putting on weight.*

Fair In some towns, including Glasgow, Paisley, and Greenock, **the Fair** is the traditional annual trades summer holiday. Each town has its own **Fair** during a particular fortnight in July or August (for example, in Glasgow, the last two weeks in July), and during these holidays many local factories and businesses close down: *the Glasgow Fair; We're going to Cyprus for the Fair.* In other parts of Scotland such holidays are known as the **Trades**.

fairin or **fairing** A **fairin** is a present from a fair. To **get one's fairin** is to get what one deserves.

fairm or **ferm** A **fairm** is a farm.

fairmer or **fermer** A **fairmer** is a farmer.

faither (rhymes with *bather*) One's **faither** is one's father: *Away ben with your faither's tea.*

fan Fan is a Northeastern form of when.

faniver (pronounced *fa-niv-er*) **Faniver** is a Northeastern form of whenever.

fank A **fank** is a sheepfold. The word comes from the Gaelic *fang* a sheepfold.

fankle To **fankle** something is to tangle it: *The fishing line had got all fankled up.* A **fankle** is a tangle or a state of confusion: *Don't get yourself in a fankle.*

fantoosh (pronounced *fan-toosh*) The word **fantoosh** means ostentatious or pretentious. The word is perhaps from the French *fantoche* a puppet.

far Far is a Northeastern form of where.

fariver (pronounced *fa-riv-er*) **Fariver** is a Northeastern form of wherever.

farl A **farl** is a three-sided oatcake or piece of shortbread made by quartering a large round one. The word derives from an older term *fardel* meaning a fourth part.

farm-toun (pronounced *farm-toon*) A farm together with its outbuildings is called a **farm-toun**.

fash To **fash** means to trouble, bother, or annoy: *Dinna fash yersel*. A **fash** is anything that is a worry, trouble, or bother.

Fatal Accident Inquiry In Scots Law a **Fatal Accident Inquiry** is a legal inquiry into a sudden or unexplained death. The English equivalent is an inquest.

fauld (pronounced *fawld*) A **fauld** is a small enclosure or pen for livestock, especially sheep.

faur (pronounced *fawr*) **Faur** means far.

faut (pronounced *fawt*) A **faut** is a fault: *It's no my faut we got beaten*. To **faut** is to fault.

feart (pronounced *feert*) or **feared** To be **feart** is to be afraid: *Away hame if ye're feart*.

feartie (pronounced *feer-tee*) or **feardie** A **feartie** is a coward: *I'm no scared of a big feartie like him*.

fecht (pronounced *feCHt*) To **fecht** is to fight or struggle. The past tense is **focht**. A **fecht** is a fight or struggle. The saying **it's a sair fecht** means life is a struggle.

fechter A **fechter** is a fighter. Someone who fights well and determinedly may be called a **bonnie fechter**.

fee Fee is an old-fashioned word meaning to hire someone, especially a farm labourer or servant.

feel A **feel** is a Northeastern word for a fool: *Better an auld man's darlin nor a young man's feel*.

feet washing Feet washing, in some parts of Scotland, is a wedding custom in which the feet of the bride or groom are ceremonially washed by friends on the night before the marriage.

feints (pronounced *faints*) In whisky production feints is the name given to the lower grade alcohol produced at the end of the second distillation. It is fed back into the process for redistillation.

fell A **fell** is a mountain, hill, or tract of upland moor: *the Campsie Fells; Goat Fell*.

Fenian The word **Fenian** is sometimes used as a derogatory term for a Roman Catholic, especially one of Irish descent. The term comes from the name of a nineteenth-century Irish nationalist group, the *Fenian* Brotherhood.

ferlie (rhymes with *early*) A **ferlie** is an old-fashioned word for a wonder, or something strange and marvellous. Something that is described as **ferlie** is wonderful or strange. The word is from the Old Norse *ferligr* meaning dreadful or monstrous.

ferm Another word for **fairm**.

fermer Another word for **fairmer**.

ferntickle (pronounced *fern-tick-l*) or **fernietickle** (pronounced *fern-ee-tick-l*) A **ferntickle** is a freckle.

feu (pronounced *few*) In Scots Law a **feu** is a right to the use of land in return for a fixed annual payment to the landowner. This payment is called **feu duty**.

feuar (pronounced *few-er*) A **feuar** is a tenant of a feu.

fey (pronounced *fay*) Someone described as **fey** is said to be fated to die or to be in a state of high spirits or unusual excitement, formerly believed to presage death.

ficher (pronounced *fiCH-er*) To **ficher** is a Northeastern word meaning to fumble or fiddle with something.

ficherie (pronounced *fiCH-er-ree*) A **ficherie** task is one which is awkward, fiddly or bothersome: a Northeastern term: *That's ower ficherie a job for me.*

fiddler's biddin' Someone who is invited at the last minute to some social occasion may be said to have had a **fiddler's biddin'**.

Fife **Fife**, sometimes referred to as **the Kingdom of Fife**, is the peninsula in East Central Scotland between the Firth of Forth and the Firth of Tay. It was formerly a county **Fife** is a former local government Region which took up most of this peninsula. It is now a single-tier local council.

Fifer A **Fifer** is a person who comes from or lives in Fife.

files In the Northeast, **files** means sometimes or occasionally. It is a local form of the Scots *whiles.*

filibeg, fillibeg or **philibeg** (pronounced *fil-lee-beg*) A **filibeg** is a kilt as worn in Highland dress. The word comes from the Gaelic term *feileadhbeag* meaning small kilt.

fin (rhymes with *tin*) In some parts of Scotland to **fin**

means to find. The past tense is **fun**: *"Where did you get that?" "Ah fun it."*

finnan haddie or **haddock** A **finnan haddie** is a smoked haddock. The word comes from a local pronunciation of *Findon*, a village in Scotland south of Aberdeen.

fire raising In Scots Law the act of deliberately setting fire to property is called **fire raising**. The English equivalent is arson.

first foot The **first foot** is the first person to enter a house in the New Year. By tradition a dark-haired man brings good luck. Another term for this is **first-footer**. To **first-foot** a house or its occupants is to visit it or them as a first foot: *After the bells we'll go and first-foot the Neilsons.*

firth A **firth** is a large inlet of the sea: *the Firth of Tay; the Cromarty Firth.* The word comes from the Old Norse *fjörthr* fjord.

fiscal Short for **procurator fiscal**.

fit ① A **fit** is a foot. The saying **a gaun fit's aye gettin** means the active and industrious are the ones who will make the most profit or progress. ② In the North of Scotland **fit** also means what. The question **fit like?** means how are you?

fite Fite is a Northeastern word meaning white.

fizz In the Glasgow area someone who looks angry may be said to have **a face like fizz**.

flair The **flair** is the floor.

flakie (pronounced *flake-ee*) To **throw a flakie** is a Glasgow expression meaning to become extremely and demonstratively angry.

flech (pronounced *fleCH*) In some parts of Scotland a **flech** is a flea.

flee To **flee** is to fly. A **flee** is a fly.

fleein (pronounced *flee-in*) The literal meaning of **fleein** is flying, but it is commonly used to mean drunk, especially in a cheerful way.

fleg To **fleg** someone is to frighten them. A **fleg** is a fright or scare.

fley (pronounced *flay*) To **fley** is to frighten or scare.

fleysome (pronounced *flay-sum*) Something described as **fleysome** is frightening.

fling A **fling** is a vigorous dance, especially the **Highland fling**.

flit To **flit** is to move house. A **flit** or **flitting** is a removal or act of moving house.

flooer (rhymes with *skewer*) A **flooer** is a flower: *Did ye no see them two wee lassies wi a' the flooers?*; *The Flooers o' the Forest*.

flow A **flow** is a marsh or swamp. It can also mean an inlet or basin of the sea, as in *Scapa Flow*.

Flow Country The **Flow Country** is an area of moorland and peat bog in northern Scotland known for its wildlife, now partially afforested.

fly for To be **fly for** something is to be smart and knowing enough to be able to deal with it. Similarly, to be **fly for** a person is to be too wise to be taken in by them.

flype To **flype** something is to turn it inside out.

flyte To **flyte** is to scold or rail at someone. A **flyte** or **flyting** is a dispute or argument. Historically, **flyting** was a competition between two poets or writers to decide which could write the most wittily abusive verse about the other. The word is still occasionally used to describe insults traded between two writers.

foo Foo is a Northeastern word meaning how.

fooiver (pronounced *foo-iv-er*) Fooiver is a Northeastern word meaning however.

foosty or **foostit** To describe something as **foosty** is to say it is mouldy: *That bread's gone foosty; a foosty smell.*

footer or **fouter** To **footer** is to potter or fiddle: *Now that I don't have to cook for a living, I find footering around in the kitchen very relaxing.* A **footer** is a person who does this. An awkward or fiddly task may also be called a **footer**.

footery or **fouterie** A **footery** task is one that is awkward or fiddly.

forby or **forbye** (pronounced *for-by*) Forby can mean besides or in addition: *There's enough for everybody and more forby.* It can also mean except: *The whole lot's here, forby one or two.*

fore If someone is described as **to the fore** this means they are alive or active: *I'm glad to hear your wee auntie's still to the fore.*

forenoon The part of a day called the **forenoon** is late morning.

foreshot In whisky distilling the **foreshot** is the first, raw spirit to be distilled. It is fed back into the process for redistillation.

forfochen (pronounced *for-foCH-en*) or **forfochtin** (pronounced *for-foCH-tin*) Someone who is **forfochen** is exhausted or worn out.

forkietail A **forkietail** is the name given in some areas to an earwig. It is sometimes shortened to **forkie**.

fornenst (pronounced *for-nenst*) If something is **fornenst** another thing it is situated against it or in front of it: *The hoose sat richt fornenst the burn.*

forrit or **furrit** (rhymes with *turret*) **Forrit** means forward: *Shift your motor forrit a bit.*

fou or **fu'** (pronounced *foo*) **Fou** means full. It can also mean drunk: *That's him gaun hame fou again.*

found (pronounced *foond*) A **found** is a foundation, especially of a building.

fouter, fouterie Variant spellings of **footer** and **footery**.

fower (rhymes with *flower*) **Fower** is the number four.

fowk (pronounced *fowk*) The word **fowk** means folk or people.

frae (pronounced *fray*) Another word for **fae**.

Free Church In Scotland the title **Free Church** generally refers to the **Free Church of Scotland** which broke away from the Church of Scotland in 1843, an event known as the **Disruption**. Those breaking away wished to form more democratic parishes that would be financed and run by parishioners and not by wealthy patrons or the Acts of Parliament that governed the Established Church. Reconciliations occurred in 1900 and 1929 when the majority of breakaway parishes either formed a union with or rejoined the Church of Scotland. The minority who refused to rejoin continued to be known as the **Free Church**. See also **Wee Free**.

freen A **freen** is a friend: *It's nae loss what a freen gets.*

fricht (pronounced *friCHt*) To **fricht** someone is to frighten them. A **fricht** is a fright.

furrit Another way of spelling **forrit**.

furth **Furth** means out, outside, or to the outside: *guests from furth of Scotland.*

fushionless (pronounced *foosh-in-liss*) A **fushionless** person is one who is physically weak or lacking in vigour or initiative.

fuskie (rhymes with *husky*) **Fuskie** is an old-fashioned Northeastern name for whisky.

fussle (rhymes with *mussel*) **Fussle** is a Northeastern word meaning whistle: *a tin fussle.*

futret (pronounced *futt-rit*) A **futret** is a North of

Scotland name for a weasel: *a wee futret-like face.* The word is a local variant of the Scots *whitrat*, ultimately from *white rat.*

fykie A **fykie** task is one involving a lot of delicate or intricate work.

gaberlunzie (pronounced *gab-ber-lunn-zee*) or **gaberlunzie-man** A **gaberlunzie** is an old-fashioned name for a tramp or wandering beggar.

gadgie (pronounced *gadge-ee*) **Gadgie** is a word meaning man, lad or chap used in much of Eastern and Northern Scotland. The word comes from Romany.

gads **Gads** is a mild expression of disgust or dismay. It is a euphemistic form of *God*.

Gael (pronounced *gale*) A **Gael** is a Celt from the parts of the Highlands and Islands of Scotland where Gaelic is, or was until recently, the mother tongue. The word comes from the Gaelic *Gaidheal*.

Gaelic (pronounced *gal-lik*) **Gaelic** is a language spoken mainly in some parts of Northwestern Scotland, particularly on Skye and the Western Isles. As a result of emigration there are also some Gaelic speakers in the Lowlands, particularly in Glasgow, and in parts of Nova Scotia. Gaelic is a Celtic language, closely related to Irish Gaelic and more distantly to Welsh and Breton. It was the main language of the Highlands until the middle of the 18th century, and a form of it was also spoken in the extreme Southwest of Scotland until the 17th century, but there are now fewer than 80 000 Gaelic speakers in Scotland. Among the Gaelic words that have been adopted into English are *galore*, *slogan*, and *cairn*. People in Scotland, particularly Gaelic speakers, often refer to the language as **the Gaelic**. To **have the Gaelic** is to be able to speak Gaelic. Something which is **Gaelic** is in Gaelic or typical of the culture of people who speak Gaelic: *Gaelic broadcasting*; *Gaelic music*.

Gaidhealtachd (pronounced *gale-taCHt*) The **Gaidhealtachd** is the area of the Highlands and Islands where Gaelic is still in everyday use.

gait An old-fashioned spelling of **gate**.

Gallovidian (pronounced *gal-lo-vid-ee-an*) A **Gallovidian** is a person from Galloway in Southwest Scotland. Something which is **Gallovidian** comes from Galloway. The word comes via Mediaeval Latin from the Welsh *Gallgwyddell* foreign, ie non-Welsh, Gaels.

Galloway (pronounced *gal-lo-way*) **Galloway** is an area of Southwest Scotland extending along the north of the Solway Firth from the River Nith at Dumfries to the West Coast. Its most south-westerly point, the **Mull of Galloway**, is the most southerly place in Scotland. A **Galloway** is a small cow of a type first bred in Galloway, either all black or black with a white band around its middle (a **belted Galloway**).

gallus (rhymes with *callous*) Someone who is **gallus** is self-confident, daring and often slightly cheeky or reckless: *He's too gallus to be intimidated by anyone.* In Glasgow the word is often used approvingly to indicate that something is noticeably stylish or impressive: *Have you seen Davie's new guitar? It's gallus!* The word was originally derogatory and meant wild, rascally and deserving to be hanged from a *gallows*.

galluses (pronounced *gal-luss-eez*) **Galluses** are braces for holding up trousers.

galshachs (pronounced *gal-shaCHs*) In the Northeast, sweets, cakes, sweet biscuits and other sweet but not necessarily healthy delicacies are referred to as **galshachs**. To eat a lot of sweets, cakes, and the like, is to **galshach intae** or **intil** them: *He's galshachin intil them.* The exact origin of the word is unclear, but it may be related to the Scots *gulsoch*, jaundice or any sickness caused by over-eating, which comes from the Old English *gule* yellow plus *sucht* illness.

galvie (pronounced *gal-vee*) **Galvie** is an informal word meaning made from galvanized iron: *a galvie bucket.*

game That's the **game** or that's the **gemme** is a Glaswegian phrase indicating that things are happening in a way intended or approved of: *Just hold it steady while I tighten the screws. Aye, that's the game!*

gang As in some northern forms of English, **gang** can mean to go, although the word is now old-fashioned or literary (it is used in many of Burns' poems). The past tense is **gaed** and the past participle **gane**.

gansey, ganzie (pronounced *gan-zee*) or **gensey**

(pronounced *genn-zee*) A **gansey** is a thick woollen jumper, especially one of the type worn by people working on fishing boats. The word is a variant of **guernsey**, another name for such a sweater.

gant To **gant** is to yawn, or to open one's mouth wide as if yawning, often with the implication of being desperate or eager for something: *Aye, you're in there. She's gantin for it.*

gantry The **gantry** in a pub or bar is the shelves or stand behind the bar where bottles of spirits are displayed. It is also a way of referring to the range of spirits, especially malt whiskies, stocked in the bar: *They've got a great gantry in here.*

gar **Gar** is an old-fashioned or literary word meaning to make or cause someone to do something, now mainly heard in the phrase *it'd gar ye grue*. (See **grue**). The past tense and participle are sometimes spelled **gart**.

gate or **gait** A **gate** is a street or path. The word is now mainly encountered as the second part of a streetname such as *Gallowgate*, *Canongate* or *Marketgait*. To **gang one's own gate** is to act as one chooses, regardless of the advice or opinion of others.

gaun (pronounced *gawn*) ① **Gaun** is a Scots form of going: *That's where we've been gaun wrang.* ② **Gaun yersel!**, which literally means "go on yourself", is a cry of encouragement: *Gaun yersel wee man!*

gaunae (pronounced *gawn-ee*) **Gaunae** means going to, either as a statement of intent or as a request: *Ah'm gaunae go for a dauner; Gaunae no make so much noise?*

gawkie (pronounced *gawk-ee*) A **gawkie** is a person who looks stupid, clumsy, or awkward. The word may be related to *gawk* to stare or gape, but its exact origin is unclear.

gawkit Someone who is **gawkit** is stupid, clumsy, or awkward-looking: *a gawkit teenager.*

gean (pronounced *geen*) A **gean** is a wild cherry or a wild cherry tree. The name comes from the Old French *guigne.*

geet (pronounced *geet*) A **geet** is a Northeastern word for a child, especially an obnoxious or illegitimate one. The word is a local variant of *get* and *git.*

geggie (pronounced *gegg-ee*) ① In the Glasgow area, the **geggie** or **geg** is the mouth, most often heard in the command *shut your geggie!* ② A **geggie** is also the name given in some areas to a child's homemade vehicle constructed from pram wheels, wooden boxes, etc. Elsewhere this is known as a **bogie**, **cairtie**, **hurlie** or **piler**.

gemme (pronounced *gemm*) A **gemme** is a game: *a gemme o fitba wi the lads.*

gemmy (pronounced *gemm-ee*) **Gemmy** is a Glaswegian word meaning bold, cheeky and spirited: *He thinks he's gemmy but he's just a tube.*

General Assembly The **General Assembly** of the Church of Scotland, or of another Presbyterian Church, is the governing body of the Church. It consists of ministers and elders representing the entire country, and is the body which supervises Church doctrine and discipline. The term is also used to refer to the annual meeting of the General Assembly of the Church of Scotland in Edinburgh.

gensey (pronounced *genn-zee*) Another name for a **gansey**.

get To **get** to do something or to go somewhere is to be able, be allowed, or manage to do it or go there: *I wanted to go to the party, but I had to visit my Grannie, so I didn't get.*

gey (pronounced *giy* or *gay*) **Gey** means very or exceptionally: *gey few; It's gey warm in here.*

gie (pronounced *gee*) To **gie** is to give: *Gie the wean a sweetie.* The past tense is **gied** and the past participle is **gien**: *She gied me a lift; He'd gien me a hard time.*

gies (pronounced *geez*) **Gies** is a shortening of **gie us** meaning give us or give me: *Gies a haun.*

gigot (pronounced *jig-ot*) A **gigot** of lamb is a leg of lamb. A **gigot chop** is a lamb chop taken from the leg. The word was originally French.

gill (pronounced *jill*) A **gill** is a unit for measuring liquid, equal to one quarter of a pint (about 142 ml). In Scottish bars, spirits were traditionally sold in measures of one fifth of a gill, although some establishments prided themselves on selling the larger measure of one quarter of a gill: *a quarter-gill pub.* These measures have been replaced by metric measures of 25 ml and 35 ml.

gillie or **ghillie** (pronounced *gill-ee*) A **gillie** is a person who is employed to act as a guide and assistant to people who are out angling or shooting. The word comes from the Gaelic *gille* a lad or servant.

gin (pronounced *ginn*) **Gin** is an old-fashioned or poetic word meaning if: *Gin he was alive the day.*

ging (pronounced *ging*) To **ging** is to go: *They're just a pack o sheep, wi'oot the guts to ging aff on their own.* The past tense and past participle can be either **gaed** or **gied**. The word is a chiefly Northeastern variant of *gang*.

ginger In the Glasgow area, a fizzy soft drink such as lemonade or limeade is often referred to informally as **ginger**.

gird (pronounced *gird*) A **gird** is an old-fashioned child's toy consisting of a metal hoop which can be rolled along the ground, often with the help of a metal or wire hook known as a **cleek**: *a gird and cleek.*

girdle A **girdle** is a thick round iron plate placed on top of a cooker, on which food such as scones and pancakes can be cooked. A **girdle scone** is a scone which has been cooked on a girdle rather than in an oven. The word is a variant of *griddle*.

girn To **girn** is to moan, complain, or grumble: *The losers were still girning and whining about the alleged injustice they had suffered; a girning wee malcontent.*

girny or **girnie** A person, especially a child, who is **girny** is irritable and constantly grumbling or whining about something.

girse (pronounced *girss*) **Girse** is grass.

glaikit or **glaiket** (pronounced *glay-kit*) **Glaikit** means silly, foolish or thoughtless. It can be used both of a person and of something someone has done: *Go and get the mop, you glaikit lump!*; *That's a glaikit way of doing it.* The origin of the word is unclear, although it is related to the old Scots word *glaiks* tricks or deceptions.

Glaswegian A **Glaswegian** is a person who comes from or lives in Glasgow, and something which is **Glaswegian** comes from or is typical of Glasgow: *a novel about a young gay Glaswegian; typical Glaswegian humour.* **Glaswegian** is also the distinctive dialect of the Glasgow area, a form of West Central Scots which has been strongly influenced by large scale immigration from Ireland and the Gaelic-speaking Highlands during the 19th and early 20th centuries. It has also lost a number of words and features found in most other forms of Scots: no-one in Glasgow says "ken" rather than "know", or "richt" rather than "right", for instance. Glaswegian is also notable for its lively rhyming slang.

glaur rhymes with (pronounced *war*) **Glaur** is soft, sticky mud.

glen A **glen** is a valley with a stream or river running through it. It is generally narrower than a **strath**. **Glen** often forms part of a place name, such as *Rouken Glen* or

Glen Moriston. The word comes from Gaelic, where it is spelt *gleann*.

Glencoe (pronounced *glen-koh*) **Glencoe** is a valley in the Southwest Highlands where, in 1692, at the instigation of the British Crown, members of the Macdonald clan were massacred by a group of Campbells and English troops.

glengarry (pronounced *glen-gar-ree*) A **glengarry** is a type of brimless cap or hat which has straight sides, a crease running from front to back at the top, and often two short ribbons hanging from the back. It is probably called after the Highland chief Macdonnell of *Glengarry* who popularized the wearing of it during the visit of King George the Fourth to Edinburgh in 1822.

Glesca (pronounced *gless-ka*) or **Glesga** (pronounced *glezz-ga*) **Glesca** is the Glasgow dialect form of Glasgow: *a Glesca keelie.* Other regions have their own dialect forms of the word, such as **Glesgie**.

Glesca screwdriver Another name for a **Paisley screwdriver**.

glessy A **glessy** is a marble made out of glass.

gloamin The **gloamin** is the period of twilight at dusk. The word, which is now mainly literary, is sometimes also used to refer to the period of twilight at dawn. It comes from Old English *glōmung*, and is related to the Old Norse *glāmr* moon.

golach (pronounced *goll-aCH*) In parts of Eastern

Scotland, a beetle is known as a **golach**. Compare **horny-golach**, an earwig. The word comes from the Gaelic *gobblag* an earwig or forked object.

goldie A **wee goldie** is an informal term for a glass of whisky.

goonie A **goonie** is a nightie or other similar gown, such as one worn by a patient going to the operating theatre in hospital.

gowan (pronounced *gow-an*) **Gowans** are daisies or, occasionally, other similar white or yellow flowers.

gowf (pronounced *gowf*) **Gowf** is another name for golf, now slightly old-fashioned, but still used in the official name of at least one golf club: *The match will take place at Loudoun Gowf Club in Galston.* A **gowfer** is a golfer: *A mad keen gowfer will play in any weather.*

go with In many parts of Scotland, to be **going with** someone is to be involved in a romantic relationship with them: *I've been going with him for four months now.*

gowk (pronounced *gowk*) A **gowk** is a cuckoo. **Gowk** can also mean a fool or simpleton. In some parts of Eastern Scotland, the victim of an April Fool's Day trick is known as an **April gowk**. The word comes from the Old Norse *gaukr*.

gowp (pronounced *gowp*) To **gowp** is to throb painfully: *Ma heid's gowpin.* The word is used in parts of Central and Southern Scotland. It is possibly imitative in origin.

graip (pronounced *grep*) A **graip** is a large metal-pronged fork used for gardening or agricultural work: *They loaded their carts graip by painful graipful.* The term comes from Old Norse, and is related to the words **grip** and **grope.**

graith (pronounced *greth*) The **graith** for a job is the equipment, tools or gear needed for it. For example, the rod and line needed for fishing, or a rock band's instruments and amplifiers, may both be described as **graith:** *fishing graith*; *Hurry up and get the graith into the van.* **Graith** was originally a verb meaning to be ready or prepare and comes from Old Norse.

gralloch (pronounced *gral-loCH*) To **gralloch** a deer is to disembowel it. The word comes from the Gaelic *greallach* intestines.

Grampian Grampian is a former local government Region in the Northeast, which occupied most of the Eastern half of Scotland from just north of Montrose to the Moray Firth. It is now administered by three single-tier local councils: Moray, Aberdeenshire, and the City of Aberdeen.

Granite City Aberdeen is nicknamed **the Granite City** because many of its buildings are made from locally-quarried granite: *Smoke drifts across the dance floor as the Granite City's young folk writhe and gyrate to a heavy beat.*

gravit (pronounced *grah-vit* or *graw-vit*) In Northern Scotland a scarf, especially a warm woollen one, is sometimes referred to as a **gravit.** The word is a variant of *cravat.*

green A **green** is an area of grassy ground attached to a house or other building, for instance the shared garden behind a block of tenement flats (the **back green**).

greet To **greet** is to cry or weep. The past tense is **grat** and the past participle is **grutten**: *What are you greetin about?* A **greet** is a period of time spent crying: *I like a good greet at the pictures now and again.* There are a number of Scots idioms derived from **greet**. When a child is or children are crying noisily and for a long time, the situation can be described as a **greetin match**. **Greetin face** is a way of referring to someone who always looks miserable. A **Greetin Teenie** is a person who is always complaining.

Gretna Green **Gretna Green** is a village at the western end of the border with England, which is famous because, in earlier days when Scottish marriage laws made it easier to wed in Scotland than in England, many couples eloped from England and got married here. Although these laws have now changed some people still regard it as a romantic place in which to get married.

grieve A **grieve** is a foreman or supervisor on a farm.

grippie **Grippie** is a Northeastern word meaning mean or miserly.

grog In the Glasgow area, to **grog** is to spit: *Paul got lifted for groggin at the polis.* A **grog** is a lump of spittle.

grosset (rhymes with *cosset*) A **grosset** is a gooseberry. The word comes from the French *groseille*.

ground In bagpipe music, a **ground** is the basic tune

played at the beginning of a **pibroch**, which is then repeated a number of times with much variation and elaboration. It is a translation of the Gaelic term *ūrlar*.

grue (pronounced *grew*) To **grue** is to shudder or shiver from fear or disgust. Something which **gars ye grue** is so frightening or horrific that it makes your blood run cold. The English word **gruesome** comes from **grue**.

gub The **gub** is an informal, slightly impolite, name for the mouth: *Shut your gub, you!* To **gub** someone is to hit or punch them on the mouth. To **gub** a person or team is to defeat them heavily: *I see Morton got gubbed again on Saturday.* A **gubbing** is a heavy defeat. The word comes from the Gaelic *gob* a beak or mouth.

guddle Any untidy or messy place or state can be described as a **guddle**. To **guddle** is to try to catch a fish, such as a trout, with one's bare hands.

guid (pronounced *gid* or *good*) Guid is a Scots word meaning good: *It's a guid pint, this.* Someone's **guid sister**, **guid son** etc. is their sister-in-law, son-in-law and so on.

guiser (pronounced *guy-zer*) A **guiser** is a person who has put on fancy dress to take part in any of various traditional events, notably at Halloween or in the **Up-Helly-Aa** festival in Shetland.

guising (pronounced *guy-zing*) Guising is a Scottish Halloween tradition in which children put on fancy dress and visit nearby houses where they sing a song or tell jokes and in return are given fruit, nuts or sweets.

gumsy (pronounced *gum-zee*) Someone who is **gumsy** has no natural teeth and, if a denture-wearer, does not have any dentures in.

gushet (pronounced *gush-it*) A **gushet** is a triangular piece of land, such as one between two roads which meet at a sharp angle.

guttered To be **guttered** is to be exceptionally drunk. The word probably comes from the image of someone being so intoxicated that they end up lying unconscious in a gutter.

gutties (rhymes with *butties*) In West Central and Southwest Scotland, plimsolls are frequently referred to as **gutties**. The term is a shortening of *gutta-percha*, a type of rubber.

gweed (pronounced *gweed*) Gweed is a Northeastern word meaning good: *She gied the press ablow the sink a gweed redd up.* It can also be used as a euphemism for God: *Gweed kens fa did it.*

gype (pronounced *gipe*) A **gype** is a Northeastern term for a foolish or stupid person. The word is related to the Old Norse *geip*.

gyperie (pronounced *gipe-er-ree*) **Gyperie** is a Northeastern word meaning foolishness.

gypit (pronounced *gipe-it*) **Gypit** is a Northeastern word meaning silly or foolish.

gyte (pronounced *gite*) **Gyte** is an old-fashioned or literary word meaning mad or crazy. To **gang gyte** is to go mad.

haar (pronounced *hahr*) A **haar** is a type of cold mist or fog from the North Sea which frequently occurs along the East coast: *The east-coast haar has lowered temperatures in Edinburgh in the morning and evening recently.* The word is of Dutch origin, coming either from Middle Dutch *hare* a biting wind, or Frisian *harig* damp.

habble A **habble** is a clumsy, not particularly successful, attempt to carry out a physical task: *He was having a habble trying to get the childproof lid off the bottle.* A **habble** is also a mess: *You've made a right habble of that bedroom.*

hack A **hack** is a crack or graze in the skin caused by cold.

hackit or **hacket** A **hackit** person is ugly. The word is most often applied to women: *I do not fancy her. She's hackit!*

hackle A **hackle** is a type of feathered ornamental badge worn in the caps of some Highland regiments.

haddie A **haddie** is a haddock. See also **finnan haddie**. A **haddie** is also a term for a clumsy or silly person: *The car's steering is so good that you have to be a real haddie to get it to misbehave.*

hae (pronounced *hay*) **Hae** means have: *I hae ma orders; Ye'll hae heard the news?*

haet (pronounced *hate*) A **haet** is the smallest amount possible, a whit or iota: *not a haet of difference.* The word was originally a contraction of the phrase *deil hae it* devil have it.

hag A **hag** can be either a swampy hollow in a moor, or a firm spot in a bog. The word is of Scandanavian origin: compare the Old Norse *högg* a gap.

haggis **Haggis** is a dish consisting of the minced liver, heart and lungs of a sheep mixed with oatmeal and suet and seasoned with salt and a liberal amount of pepper. It was traditionally cooked by boiling it in a sheep's stomach. The word probably derives from the old English verb *haggen* to hack or chop, although its exact origin is unclear.

hail ① A **hail** is another name for a goal at shinty: *Kingussie beat Kyles Athletic by six hails to two in the play-off.* ② A variant spelling of **hale**.

hain (rhymes with *rain*) To **hain** something is a Northeastern word meaning to save it for possible future use: *He's haint aa the pokes he got fae the supermairket.* The term comes from the Old Norse *hegna* to hedge or protect.

hairst (pronounced *hairst*) The **hairst** is the harvest, or the time of year in late Autumn when the harvest takes place: *farm workers at the hairst.*

hairy A **hairy** is a derogatory name for a young working-class woman, with the implication that she is tough, sluttish, or both: *A hard-faced wee hairy with a neck covered with lovebites.* The most likely derivation of the term is that such women were too poor to be able to afford hats in the days when hats were almost universally worn.

haiver A variant spelling of **haver.**

hale or **hail** The **hale** of something is all of it: *the hale winter long; the hail clanjamfrie.* See also **the hale jing-bang** at **jing-bang.** The word is from the Old English *hæl* whole.

hallirackit (pronounced *hal-lee-rack-it*) Someone who is **hallirackit** is wild, rowdy and irresponsible. This North of Scotland word is mainly used of women: *She's a damned hallirackit bitch.* The term ultimately comes from the Old Scots *halok* a silly thoughtless girl.

hame Hame means home: *Ah'm away hame; It's nothin to write hame aboot.*

hameldaeme (pronounced *hay-mel-day-mee*) **Hameldaeme** is a jocular Glaswegian saying used by someone who is going to stay at home as a reply to an enquiry about where one is going on holiday. The word is a contraction of the Glasgow pronunciation of *home will do me.*

hamesucken (pronounced *hame-suck-en*) **Hamesucken** is the crime of assaulting a person in their own home after forcing an entry in order to carry out the attack: *In a trial for hamesucken, it is difficult to prove that the intention was* *violence rather than, say, theft.* The term comes from the Old English *hāmsōcn*, from *hām* home plus *sōcn* seeking or assault.

hander or **hauner** In West Central Scotland, to **hander** someone is to help them in a fight by joining in on their side: *If thae heidbangers are waiting outside, we'll hander you.* A **hander** is a person who takes part in a fight to help someone else: *We thought he'd gone, but he came back with handers.*

handless or **haunless** Someone who is **handless** is incompetent and clumsy at any practical task involving manual dexterity: *Most wives of lawyers, professors, and the like become resigned to the fact that their husbands are handless.*

handsel (pronounced *hance-el*) A **handsel** is a gift given to someone to bring them luck at the beginning of something, for instance when they have just moved to a new house. To **handsel** someone is to give them such a gift. The word is from the Old English *handselen* delivery into the hand.

hap To **hap** is to cover or wrap: *distant hills happed in mist.* To **hap up** is to wrap up or dress warmly for protection from the cold: *well happed up against the cold.* A **hap** is a protective covering, such as a heavy coat: *That's a good warm hap you've got there.*

harl To **harl** the outer walls of a building is to cover them with a mixture of lime and gravel or small stones, to roughcast them: *a small development of harled council houses.* **Harl** or **harling** is also the name given to the mixture of lime and gravel used in covering walls in this way: *The white Skye marble which, ground into chips, provided the harl finish to houses in the north.*

Harry Wraggs The **Harry Wraggs** is a nickname occasionally used for Partick Thistle football team. It is rhyming slang for the more common *Jags*. *Harry Wragg* was a jockey.

hash To **hash** is to move about or do something in a hasty, clumsy or flustered way: *Diesel cars will take a lot of low-speed hashing about without stalling.*

haud (pronounced *hawd*) To **haud** is to hold: *She grabbed haud o me; Haud on and Ah'll chum you up the road.* The past participle is **hudden** or **hauden**.

hauf (pronounced *hawf*) **Hauf** means half: *a hauf-loaf; hauf deid.* A **hauf** is a small glass of whisky. It originally consisted of half a gill, and a **wee hauf** was a quarter-gill, but both terms are now used more loosely to mean any smallish measure: *There's a guy having a fly hauf in the toilets.* A **hauf an a hauf** is a whisky served with a half-pint of beer as a chaser.

haugh (pronounced *hawCH*) or *haw* A **haugh** is an area of meadowland beside a river. The word occurs in many place names, for instance *Flesher's Haugh, Philiphaugh* and *Haugh of Urr.* **Haugh** comes from the Old English *healh* a corner of land.

haun (pronounced *hawn*) **Haun** means hand, both as a noun and a verb: *Gies a haun wi this; Haun us ower the paper.*

hauner (pronounced *hawn-er*) Same as **hander**.

haunle (pronounced *hawn-el*) A **haunle** is a handle. To **haunle** something is to handle it.

haunless (pronounced *hawn-less*) Same as **handless**.

haver or **haiver** (pronounced *hay-ver*) To **haver** is to talk nonsense: *What's he havering about?* To describe what someone is saying as **havers** is to say that they are talking nonsense: *Don't give me your havers!*

head See **heid** for various idioms involving the word **head**.

header or **heider** A **header** is a Glaswegian word for a dangerously wild or crazy person. The word is a shortened form of *headcase*.

heart roasted In the Glasgow area, to be **heart roasted** by something, is to be greatly tormented, frustrated or worried by it.

heather Heather is a type of low-growing shrub that grows in low masses on open ground such as moorland and hillsides. It has small, typically pinkish-purple, bell-shaped flowers. The rarer **white heather** is considered by some to be lucky Something which **sets the heather on fire** or **alight** causes a great sensation or excitement: *Their results have not set the heather on fire recently.*

heavy Heavy is a type of beer similar to but slightly weaker and lighter in colour than export. The nearest English equivalent is bitter. Compare **wee heavy**.

Hebridean A **Hebridean** person or thing belongs to, is from, or is associated with the Hebrides: *the Hebridean island of Gigha; an Ayrshire man of Hebridean descent.*

Hebrides The **Hebrides** are a group of over 500 islands off the West coast of Scotland, which are separated by a wide channel into the **Inner Hebrides** which lie nearer the mainland and include the islands of Islay, Jura, Mull, Tiree, Iona and Skye among many others, and the **Outer Hebrides** which lie further out in the Atlantic and include the islands of Lewis with Harris, North Uist, Benbecula, South Uist, and Barra among others. See also **Western Isles**.

heck A **heck** is a frame or rack, especially one in a byre or stable, at the height of an animal's head, in which fodder such as hay or straw is placed.

heedrum-hodrum (pronounced *hee-drum-hoe-drum*) Lowlanders who do not understand or appreciate traditional Gaelic singing or music sometimes derogatorily refer to it as **heedrum-hodrum** or **heedrum-hodrums**: *Every Hogmanay we're expected to sit through all this heedrum-hodrum on the telly.* The term is an attempt to imitate the alleged sound of such music.

heehaw (pronounced *hee-haw*) **Heehaw** is a Glaswegian slang term meaning not the slightest bit or nothing at all: *You'll get heehaw sense out of him; Keep out of it, you. You know heehaw about it.* It is euphemistic rhyming slang for *fuck a'.*

heid (pronounced *heed*) The **heid** is the head: *She fell and banged her heid; He's aff his heid.* The **heid** or **head** of

something is its highest part: *the heid o the brae; Townhead.*
To **heid** something, especially a football, is to head it:
He heided it into the back of the net. **Heid-the-baw** is a
nickname for anyone you know, usually reasonably
affectionate if patronising, but sometimes implying
stupidity: *Here comes wee heid-the-baw now.* To get or be
given **your head in your hands to play with** is to be
punished severely: *Ye'll get your heid in your hands to play wi if
the boss sees you doing that.* To **stick the heid on** someone is
to headbutt them. **Away and bile yer heid!** is an
expression of dismissal. See also **away.**

heidbanger (pronounced *heed-bang-er*) A **heidbanger**
is a wild or crazy person: *You'll need to watch that guy, he's a
real heidbanger; The nationalist movement has its fair share of
heidbangers.*

heid billydackus (pronounced *bill-lee-dack-us*) or
heid pilliedacus (pronounced *pill-ee-dack-us*) In some
parts of Eastern Scotland, the person in charge of
something is jocularly or derogatorily referred to as the
heid billydackus. The word possibly comes from *billy,*
an old word for a man or a workmate, plus a mock Latin
ending.

heid bummer See **bummer.**

heider (pronounced *heed-er*) Same as **header.**

heidie (rhymes with *beady*) The **heidie** is an informal
name for the head teacher of a school: *the heidie of an
Ayrshire secondary school.* To **heidie** or **heidy** a football is to
play it with one's head: *He heidied it over the bar.* A **heidie**
is an instance of playing a football with the head.

Hell When someone says **Hell mend you!** (or **him, her, them, etc.**), this is an expression of extreme exasperation indicating that the speaker has given up trying to persuade the specified person about the likely dire consequences of their actions.

hems To **put the hems on** something is to control, restrain or put a stop to it: *The rain put the hems on our trip to the seaside.* To **put the hems on** someone is to make them behave in a more restrained or moderate way: *She used to go out with her pals every night, but having that wean's really put the hems on her.* A *hem* or *haim* was part of the collar put on a horse which was to be used for ploughing or pulling a cart.

hen In parts of Central and Southern Scotland, the term **hen** is used informally to address any woman or girl: *I didn't mean it that way, hen.*

herself or **hersel** The most important woman in a household, workplace, etc., such as the wife or boss, is sometimes referred to as **herself**: *Is herself at home?*

hert The **hert** is the heart: *It's no ma hert that's the problem, ken, it's ma lungs.*

het ① **Het** means hot: *You're like a hen on a het girdle.* ② In some areas, the person doing the chasing in a game like **tig** is known as **het**: *You're het!*

heuch (pronounced *hyooCH* or *hooCH*) A **heuch** is a cry of enthusiasm of the type sometimes uttered when dancing a lively dance such as a reel. To **heuch** is to give such a cry. The word is onomatopoeic.

heuchter-teuchter (pronounced *byooCH-ter-chooCH-ter* or *hooCH-ter-chooCH-ter*) **Heuchter-teuchter** is a derogatory adjective used to describe Scottish folk and country dance music by people who do not like it: *heuchter-teuchter music*. The term is based on a combination of **heuch** and **teuchter** a mildly derogatory word for a Highlander.

Hibee (pronounced *high-bee* or *hib-bee*) A **Hibee** is a supporter of Hibernian football club, who are nicknamed **the Hibees**: *As well as being a promising writer, he is also a fanatical Hibee; For years the Hibees were unable to win an Edinburgh derby no matter how well they played.*

Hielan (pronounced *heel-an*) Something or someone **Hielan** comes from or is found in the Highlands: *Munro's much-loved stories about a daft Hielan skipper and a crabbit engineer.* In some parts of the Lowlands, **Hielan** is used to mean naive, gullible or a bit stupid: *That's a Hielan way of doing things; Ye'll no fool me — I'm no sae Hielan.*

Hielanman (pronounced *heel-an-man*) A **Hielanman** is a rather old-fashioned word for a man from the Highlands, a Highlander.

High Court The **High Court**, or the **High Court of Justiciary** to give it its full name, is the supreme criminal court in Scotland, which handles all cases of murder or rape and all other cases involving potential heavy penalties. High Court trials are heard in a number of towns including Glasgow, Edinburgh, Kilmarnock, Inverness, Kirkcaldy, Stonehaven and Dunfermline: *He* *was jailed for six years at the High Court in Paisley; The case was sent to the High Court after a Glasgow sheriff decided his maximum sentencing power of three years was inadequate.*

high doh To be **up to high doh** is to be in a state of extreme agitation or excitement: *The kids were up to high doh because they knew Santa would be coming.*

Higher A **Higher** is an exam or qualification at the more advanced level of the Scottish Certificate of Education, usually taken at the end of the Fifth Year in a secondary school, ie at the age of 16 or 17. An individual **Higher** is not as advanced as an A Level, but Scottish students generally sit more Highers in a wider range of subjects than their counterparts elsewhere in Britain: *She left school with five Highers; Higher Physics.* Compare **CSYS** and **Standard Grade**.

high heid yin (pronounced *high heed yin*) A **high heid yin** is a person in a position of power or authority: *Politicians, journalists and academics — opinion-shaping high heid yins in general.*

High Kirk The **High Kirk** is the main Church of Scotland church in a town or area. Technically there is no such thing as a "cathedral" in the Church of Scotland, and the churches generally known as "Glasgow Cathedral" and "St Giles Cathedral" are strictly *the High Kirk of Glasgow* and *the High Kirk of St Giles.*

Highland ① Something or someone **Highland** comes from, is found in or is typical of the Scottish Highlands: *a narrow Highland road; It's an important but little-*

known piece of Highland history. ② **Highland** malt whisky is malt whisky produced in any part of the Scottish Highlands other than Speyside, Islay or the Campbeltown area of south Kintyre. ③ **Highland** is a former local government Region and now a single-tier local council. It administers most of Northwest Scotland, including the area of the mainland lying roughly north of Mull and west of Forres and the more northerly of the Inner Hebrides.

Highland cattle Highland cattle are cattle belonging to a breed with shaggy, usually reddish-brown hair, and long horns.

Highland dress Highland dress is a form of men's formal dress based on traditional Highland wear, consisting of a kilt and sporran, short black jacket over a frilled white shirt, and long socks with a skean-dhu carried in the right sock.

Highlander A **Highlander** is a person from the Highlands: *Many young Highlanders are forced to leave the area to find work.*

Highland fling A **Highland fling** is a type of vigorous dance for one person.

Highland Games A **Highland Games** is an event at which competitions in sports, piping and dancing are held. Many of the sporting contests, such as tossing the caber or throwing the hammer are of a type traditionally associated with the Highlands, but **Highland Games** are also held in many parts of the Lowlands: *Shotts Highland Games.*

Highlands Geographically, **the Highlands** is a name for the largely mountainous part of Scotland lying north of the geological fault line which runs between near Dumbarton and near Stonehaven. Socially, **the Highlands** refers to the smaller mountainous area in the Northwest of Scotland which was the historical homeland of Gaelic culture, and does not include Aberdeenshire or the coastal region east of Inverness.

Highlands and Islands The phrase **the Highlands and Islands** usually refers to the Highlands of mainland Scotland plus the Western Isles, but not Orkney or Shetland: *Environmentalists were accused of wishing to keep Shetland and the Highlands and Islands as poor and underdeveloped regions.* In a few cases, the term does include Orkney and Shetland: *the Euro MP for the Highlands and Islands.*

himself or **himsel** The most important man in a household, workplace, etc., such as the husband or boss, is sometimes referred to as **himself**: *Here's himself now.*

hine (rhymes with *mine*) In parts of North and East Scotland, to go or be **hine** or **hine awa** is to go or be far away: *hine ayont the braes; They'll be hine awa.*

hin-end (pronounced *hin-end* or *hin-en*) The **hin-end** of something is the back, rear, or last section of it. The **hin-end** also means the human buttocks: *You might tidy up your stuff instead of leaving it all at your hin-end.*

hing To **hing** is to hang: *cobwebs hinging fae the ceiling* To **hing** is also to lean out of a window to watch the world go by, chat to neighbours, etc. A **hing** is a period of time spent leaning out of a window to watch what is happening in the street, talk to neighbours, etc: *Ah wis jist havin a hing when Ah saw the polis gaun up the close opposite.*

hingy (rhymes with *clingy*) If someone, particularly a child, is slightly unwell and looking for sympathy or attention, they can be described as **hingy**: *Jordan's been a bit hingy all day.* The word alludes to the image of a sick child hanging on to a parent.

hinna or **hinnae** (rhymes with *whinny*) In some parts of Scotland **hinna** means haven't: *They hinna got ony good tatties.*

hippin A **hippin** is a towelling nappy for a baby. The word is falling into disuse as towelling nappies are gradually being superseded by disposable ones. A **hippin** is so called because it covers a baby's **hips** (as well as other, potentially messier, parts).

hirple (pronounced *hirp-l*) To **hirple** is to limp: *He hirpled off injured midway through the second half.* A **hirple** is a limp.

hit in In shinty, a team takes a **hit in** if their opponents accidentally put the ball over the sidelines of the pitch. The player taking the hit in throws the ball up in the air and hits it with the heel of the **caman** (shinty stick). A goal can be scored directly from a hit in.

hoast A **hoast** is a cough. To **hoast** is to cough.

hoatching If a place is **hoatching** it is very busy or crowded: *Largs is always hoatching on a holiday Monday.* If a place is **hoatching with** something, it is full of or infested by it or them: *The island was hoatching with midges.*

hochmagandy (pronounced *hoCH-ma-gan-dee*) or **houghmagandie** Hochmagandy is a jocular or poetic word for sexual intercourse, for recreation not procreation, between people who are not married to each other: *Ye cannae beat a bit of the old hochmagandy.* The origin of the term is not clear, but the first part of it probably comes from *hough*, the thigh.

hodden Hodden is a type of old-fashioned coarse homespun cloth. **Hodden grey** is a form of it made from a mixture of black and white wool: *a hodden grey suit.*

hogg or **hogget** A hogg is not a pig but a young sheep, less than one year old, which has been weaned but not yet sheared.

Hogmanay (pronounced *hog-ma-nay* or *hug-ma-nay*) Hogmanay is the 31st of December, New Year's Eve: *BBC Scotland's Hogmanay show, Hogmanay Live, was watched by 1.2 million viewers.* The word ultimately comes from the Old French *aguillanneuf* a New Year's Eve gift.

homologate (pronounced *hom-moll-o-gate*) To **homologate** a decision is to confirm or ratify it at a later date. The word is usually used when a committee or the officials of an organization have made a decision which then has to be put to the full membership to make it valid: *It was quite normal for emergency action to be taken by the officials and committee chairmen and for that action to be homologated later by the council.* The word comes via

Medieval Latin from the Greek *homolegein* to approve, from *homos* same plus *legein* to speak.

Honest Men Ayr United football team are nicknamed **the Honest Men**. The name refers to Burns' description of Ayr as a place "ne'er a town surpasses / For honest men and bonnie lasses" in "Tam O' Shanter".

hoodie A **hoodie** is a hooded crow, a subspecies of carrion crow which has a grey body and a black head, tail and wings. The word is sometimes extended to refer to any carrion crow.

hoolet A **hoolet** is an owl The term comes from the French *hulotte* an owl.

hooley A **hooley** is a wild party. The word was originally Irish, but is also used in some parts of Scotland.

hoor ① (pronounced *hoo-er* or *hoor*) A **hoor** or **hure** is, literally, a prostitute; but the word is more often used as an offensive term of abuse for any woman: *He's running around wi some wee hoor fae Fife; Shut up, ye auld hoor!* **Hoor** is also used as a general term of abuse for any unpleasant person or thing: *We'd a hoor o a job gettin it clean.* The word is a Scots form of *whore.* ② (pronounced *oor*) An **hoor** is an hour: *She's been in her bed the last hoor-an-a-half.*

hoormaister (pronounced *hoor-may-ster*) A **hoor-maister** is a sexually promiscuous man.

hoose (rhymes with *moose*) A **hoose** is a house: *Come ben the hoose.*

horny-golach (pronounced *horn-ee-goll-aCH*) A **horny-golach** is the name given in some areas, particularly the Northeast, to an earwig. Compare **golach**. *Golach* comes from the Gaelic *gobhlag* meaning an earwig or forked object.

hough (pronounced *hawCH*) A **hough** of ham, beef, etc. is a joint cut from the shin of the pig or cow. See also **pottit hough**. The word comes from the Old English *bōh* meaning heel.

houghmagandie (pronounced *hawCH-ma-gan-dee*) Another way of spelling **hochmagandy**.

how How can, confusingly, mean why: *How did you no tell me?* **How no** means why not: *Why them, how no us?*; *She said Ah couldnae go, but she didnae say how no.*

howe (pronounced *bow*) A **howe** is a depression or hollow in the landscape, an area of low-lying land surrounded by hills. The word is sometimes used in place names: *the Howe of Fife.*

howff (pronounced *bowf*) A **howff** is somewhere, especially a pub, used as a regular meeting place: *a lively musical howff with excellent real ale.* The word probably comes from the Dutch or Flemish *hof* a courtyard or enclosed space.

howk (pronounced *bowk*) To **howk** something is to extract it by, or as if by, digging or scraping: *We saw a few locals exercising their right to howk for cockles by hand and bucket; ballads howked from a spare and hostile landscape.* See also **tattie howkin**. *Howk* comes from an old Low German word *bolken* meaning to dig or hollow out.

howtowdie (pronounced *how-tow-dee*) Howtowdie is a dish consisting of boiled chicken with spinach and poached eggs. The word, which formerly also referred to a young chicken or pullet suitable for boiling, comes from the Old French *bétoudeau* or *estaudeau* a fat young chicken for cooking.

huckle To **huckle** is a Glasgow word meaning to force someone to move by manhandling them or bundling them roughly. It is always followed by a word indicating direction, such as *into*, *out* or *away*: *The bouncers huckled him out before any real trouble started.*

hudderie Someone who is **hudderie** is untidily or scruffily dressed.

hudgie When a Glaswegian child **takes** or **catches a hudgie**, they hang on to the back of a moving lorry and get carried along by it.

humph To **humph** something heavy is to carry or lug it: *The main problem with living in a top flat is having to humph your messages up three flights of stairs.* If an idea **comes up your humph**, it suddenly occurs to you. Someone who is **humphie** or **humphie-backit** has a hunchback.

Hun A **Hun** is a derogatory name for a Rangers supporter: *Every non-Hun in Scotland will have welcomed Rangers' cup defeat.* Rangers football club is derogatorily known as **the Huns**.

hunner A **hunner** is a hundred: *There's hunners o them.*

hurdies The **hurdies** of a person or animal are the buttocks and hips: *sturdy hurdies.*

hure (pronounced *hoo-er* or *hoor*) A variant spelling of **hoor** (whore).

hurl A **hurl** is a lift or journey in a car or other motor vehicle: *Any chance of a hurl into town?*

hurlie A **hurlie** is the name given in some areas to a child's homemade vehicle constructed from pram wheels, wooden boxes, etc. Elsewhere this is known as a **bogie**, **cairtie**, **geggie** or **piler**.

hut **Hut** is a broad Scots form of hit: *He hut me, Miss!*

-ie The diminutive ending **-ie** is commonly attached to words, often implying informality rather than smallness, as in *mannie*, *bittie* or *sweetie*.

ilk ① The word **ilk** is used in personal titles to indicate that the person named is proprietor or laird of the place named: *Moncrieffe of that ilk*. ② **Ilk** can also mean each or every: *It's grand to be waukin ilk day and find yourself nearer to Islay*.

ilka **Ilka** is an old-fashioned or literary word meaning each or every one: *There's a dub at ilka door*.

ill-trickit (pronounced *ill-trick-it*) **Ill-trickit** is a Northeastern word which means naughty or mischievous: *an ill-trickit bairn*.

inby (pronounced *in-buy*) **Inby** means inside or into the house: *If the rain comes on take the washin inby*.

inch ① An **inch** is a small island. The word is often found as part of place names, such as *Inchmurrin* or *Inch Kenneth*. ② **Inch** can also mean an area of low-lying land beside a river. Again it is a common component of place names, such as *Markinch* or *the North Inch*. Both senses of the word come from the Gaelic *innis* an island.

induct To **induct** a person is to formally install them as minister of a particular church: *The Rev. Marjory Maclean is to be inducted on March 26 as the minister of the Church of Scotland in Stromness.* An **induction** is a church service in which a minister is ceremonially installed.

ingin or **ingan** (pronounced *ing-in*) An **ingin** is an onion: *See's two pun o' ingins.*

interdict In Scots Law an **interdict** is a court order banning something until a court has decided whether or not it is legal. The English equivalent is an injunction: *Councillor Marshall sought an interim interdict to prevent the rave taking place.*

intimations **Intimations** are formal announcements of past events such as deaths, births, or engagements, or of future events such as marriages. These may be read out in church or printed in a newspaper.

intimmers (pronounced *in-tim-merz*) The **intimmers** are the insides. The word, which is most common in the North and East, can be used either of the internal workings of a mechanical device such as a clock or engine or, jocularly, of the human stomach and intestines. It originally referred to the internal *timbers* of a ship's hull.

Inverness-shire (pronounced *in-ver-ness-sher* or *in-ver-ness-shire*) **Inverness-shire** is a former county in Northwestern Scotland, consisting of a large area of the Northwestern mainland and many islands including Skye and the southern part of the Western Isles. It is now administered by Highland single-tier local council.

Iron Brew (pronounced *eye-rin*) **Iron Brew** is a popular orange-coloured carbonated soft drink. It is popularly supposed to have hangover-curing properties. The spelling **Irn Bru** is a trademark.

Islands Council An **Islands Council** is any of the three divisions (Orkney, Shetland, and the Western Isles) into which Scottish islands are divided for purposes of local government. They were kept intact in the local government changes of 1996 that saw the demise of both **Regions** and **Districts**.

Islay (pronounced *iy-la*) An **Islay** malt whisky is one produced on the island of Islay at the southern end of the Inner Hebrides. They are amongst the peatiest flavoured of all Scottish malts.

isnae (pronounced *iz-nee*) or **isna** (pronounced *iz-na*) **Isnae** means is not: *He is but she isnae; The phone isnae workin.*

-it -it is a verb ending used in Scots to make the past tense, as in *wastit* or *roastit.*

ither (rhymes with *dither*) **Ither** means other: *No that yin, the ither yin.*

j The letter **j** is often pronounced to rhyme with "buy" rather than "bay".

jag To **jag** something is to prick it: *He jagged his hand on the barbed wire*. A **jag** is an instance of this. It can also mean an injection: *The wean got a jag at school the day*. Football teams with the word "Thistle" in their names are often nicknamed **the Jags**, most notably Partick Thistle.

jaggy Something that is **jaggy** is prickly or pointed: *the narrow road between these dark jaggy heights*. A **jaggy** is also a stinging nettle.

jaicket (pronounced *jay-kit*) A **jaicket** is a jacket. **One's jaicket is on a shoogly nail.** See **shoogly**.

jakie (rhymes with *flaky*) In the Glasgow area **jakie** is a slang term for an alcoholic down-and-out.

jalouse (pronounced *ja-looz*) To **jalouse** is to suspect or infer: *I jaloused ye'd be wantin yer tea*.

Jambo (pronounced *jam-boh*) A **Jambo** is a nickname for a supporter of Heart of Midlothian football team, one of whose nicknames is **the Jambos**: *Any time the Jambos string a few good results together half the folk in Edinburgh* *suddenly claim they've always been Hearts fans.* The word comes from *Jam Tarts* (see below).

Jam Tarts Heart of Midlothian football team is nicknamed **the Jam Tarts**. The term is rhyming slang for *Hearts*, the informal name for the club, and probably also influenced by the traditional maroon colour of the team's shirts.

jannie A **jannie** is a school janitor or caretaker.

jaup (rhymes with *gawp*) To **jaup** is to splash or spatter. A **jaup** is a splash or spilt drop: *jaups of paint*. The word is onomatopoeic.

jaur (rhymes with *war*) A **jaur** is a jar: *See if ye can get the lid aff this jaur.*

jawbox A **jawbox** is a kitchen sink. The word may come from the Scots *jaw* meaning to splash or pour.

jeelie or **jeely** (rhymes with *mealy*) **Jeelie** means jelly or jam: *My gran used to give me jeelie pieces for my lunch.* A **jeelie-jaur** is a jamjar.

jeelie pan A **jeelie pan** is a pan used in making jelly or jam.

jenny A **tea jenny** is someone, of either sex, who drinks a lot of tea.

jenny-a'-things (pronounced *jen-nee-aw-things*) A **jenny-a'-things** is a small shop selling a wide variety of goods.

jenny longlegs A **jenny longlegs** is a crane fly: *Daddy, there's a big jenny longlegs in my bedroom.*

jerseys To **sell the jerseys** means to betray a cause: *Our so-called representatives have gone and sold the jerseys again.* The phrase comes from football where it is said of players who don't appear to be trying hard that they have **sold the jerseys**.

jessie A **jessie** is an effeminate, weak, or cowardly man: *What are ye greetin for, ye big jessie?*; *Shinty is not a game for jessies.*

jiggered To be **jiggered** is to be exhausted or tired out: *You come home jiggered some days, but the work's not so bad.*

jiggin Jiggin is dancing or a dance: *Who's all comin tae the jiggin?*

Jim or **Jimmy** In the Glasgow area the name **Jim** or **Jimmy** is used informally to address any man not known to the speaker: *Got the right time, Jim?*

jing-bang (pronounced *jing-bang*) The **hail jing-bang** means the whole lot or everything.

jings Jings is a mild exclamation: *Jings! I didn't know we weren't supposed to sit here.*

jink To **jink** is to move swiftly or jerkily or make a quick turn in order to dodge: *He jinked through from 20 metres out for a superb individual try.*

Jock Jock is a slang word or term of address for a Scot. Many Scots, however, find these usages offensive.

Jock Tamson's bairns The saying **we're a' Jock Tamson's bairns** means that everyone shares the same humanity and that no one person is innately better than another.

joco (pronounced *jo-ko*) To be **joco** is to be happy, relaxed, and self-satisfied.

jorrie (rhymes with *lorry*) A **jorrie** is a marble: *Who's for a game o' jorries?*

jotter A **jotter** is a school exercise book: *She wrote about the birthday party in her news jotter.* To **get one's jotters** means to be sacked from a job: *The proprietor thought too highly of the hard-working young man to give him his jotters.*

jouk (rhymes with *book*) To **jouk** is to duck or dodge: *She jouked out the way of the snowball.* A **jouk** is a sudden evasive movement.

junior A **junior** football team is a non-league side, affiliated to the Scottish Junior Football Association rather than the SFA. Such teams are collectively known as **the juniors**: *He played junior football for a couple of years after his injury; The Junior Cup Final will again be shown live on TV this year.*

kail or **kale Kail** is a type of cabbage or any dish made from cabbage, particularly a vegetable broth or stew. **Kail** also means food in general. This now old-fashioned sense of the word derives from the fact that **kail** was once one of the staple foods of the Scottish diet: *I will be back here to my kail against ane o'clock*. The phrase **cauld kail het again** in its literal sense means yesterday's leftover food reheated and served again. It is also used figuratively to mean a story that one has heard countless times before. **Kail** is the Scots form of *cole*.

kailyard or **kaleyard** A **kailyard** is a vegetable patch or kitchen garden. **Kailyard** is also used to allude to an unrealistically sentimental and couthy picture of Scottish life similar to that which the writers of the **Kailyard School** are often accused of displaying: *the decayed romanticism of tartanry and kailyard*.

Kailyard School or **Kaleyard School** The **Kailyard School** is the name given to a group of Scottish writers who depicted rural life in Scotland in the late nineteenth and early twentieth centuries. Such writers, of whom J.M. Barrie is the most famous, used authentic dialect in their works but tended to paint a rather idealized or sentimental portrait of country life.

131   **keech**

keech (pronounced *keeCH*) Keech is excrement.

keek To **keek** is to peep or glance at something: *She keeked out through the curtains.* A **keek** is also a peep or a glance: *Take a keek out of the window.* The word is from the Middle Dutch *kīken* to look.

keeker A **keeker** is a black eye: *I had a right keeker the next morning.* The word is from **keek**.

keekhole A **keekhole** is a peephole or a chink in a door or wall.

keelie (rhymes with *steely*) ① A **keelie** is a young working-class male from a city or large town. The term is generally derogatory and implies that the person is rough, tough, and a potential hooligan. In Glasgow, however, it is sometimes used more neutrally. Also in Glasgow girls can be called **keelies**: *a Glesca keelie.* The word comes from the Gaelic *gille* a lad. ② A **keelie** is also an old-fashioned name for a kestrel. This sense is probably imitative of the bird's cry.

keepie-uppie (pronounced *keep-e-up-ee*) Keepie-uppie is the skill of juggling with a football with one's feet, knees, chest, and head.

kelpie In Scottish folklore, a **kelpie** is a water spirit or demon in the form of a horse. **Kelpies** were believed to inhabit lochs and rivers, and to lure the unwary to watery graves. **Kelpie** is possibly from the Gaelic *cailpeach* a bullock.

Kelvinside (pronounced *kel-vin-side*) A **Kelvinside**

accent is an affected and over-refined form of Scottish English spoken by some of the genteel upper-middle class inhabitants of the Glasgow area. It is named after a wealthy residential area in the West End of Glasgow One of the characteristics of the Kelvinside accent is the pronunciation of "ah" as "eh": *These little French fencies are ectually rether nice.* In Edinburgh the equivalent accent is known as **Morningside**.

ken To **ken** is to know. The past tense and past participle is **kent**. The word is in frequent everyday use everywhere in Scotland, with the exception of the Glasgow area: *I kent I'd find ye here; D'ye ken wee Quigley fae Darvel?; It's nice to see a weel-kent face.* **Ken** is also used as a filler word to make a pause in speaking or add slight emphasis to a statement in the same way as `you know': *Mickey Weir's no playin' for the Hibs the day, ken.* The word ultimately derives from the Old Norse **kenna** to perceive.

kenspeckle Kenspeckle means familiar, well-known, or easily recognized: *He is a kenspeckle figure in Glasgow's Asian community.* The word perhaps comes from the Old Norse **kennispecki** power of recognition.

kep Kep is a now chiefly Northeastern word meaning to catch: *He keppit the ba.* It can also mean to catch a bus or train: *I keppit e bus at e heid o e road.* The word comes from an obsolete sense of **keep**, to put oneself in the way of.

keys In children's games a cry of **keys!** indicates the speaker's desire for a truce or a temporary suspension of the rules. The word is chiefly found in Western Scotland, children in the East generally using the term **barley** instead.

kick To say that someone **kicks with the left foot** is a humorous way of saying that the person is a Catholic. Someone described as **kicking with the wrong foot** professes a different religion from that of the speaker. This phrase is used especially by Protestants of Catholics and vice versa. Scottish members of non-Christian religions have yet to be heard employing this expression. The terms allude to the belief in the North of Ireland that Catholic farm workers use their left foot to push the spade when digging, and Protestants the right.

Killie Kilmarnock football team is nicknamed **Killie**: *Killie's victory was all the more remarkable in that they achieved it with ten men.*

Kilmarnock bonnet (pronounced *kill-mar-nock bun-it*) A **Kilmarnock bonnet** is a flat broad cap made of blue, red, or black wool. This type of cap was produced in Kilmarnock, an Ayrshire town once noted for its textile industries.

kilt A **kilt** is a knee-length pleated skirt, especially one in tartan, worn as part of a man's **Highland dress**. Originally worn in the Highlands and then by Scottish regiments in the British Army, **kilts** are now to be seen adorning Scotsmen (whether Highlanders or Lowlanders) at weddings, graduations, and other celebratory occasions. The word comes from the Danish *kilte* to tuck up.

kiltie A **kiltie** is a jocular and slightly derogatory word used to describe a man wearing a kilt.

Kincardine (pronounced *kin-card-in*) **Kincardine** or **Kincardineshire** is a former county in Northeastern Scotland, on the East Coast south of Aberdeen. It is now administered by Aberdeenshire single-tier local council. It is also known as **the Mearns**.

Kinross (pronounced *kin-ross*) **Kinross** or **Kinross-shire** is a former county of Eastern Scotland, inland from Fife. It is now administered by Perthshire and Kinross single-tier local council.

kirk A **kirk** is a Presbyterian church: *a small local country kirk*; *Off she went to kirk*. It is sometimes used, with an initial capital, in the name of individual churches: *Bothkennar Kirk near Falkirk*. The word derives from the Old Norse *kirkja*.

Kirk The **Kirk** is a less formal name for the Church of Scotland: *He is the convenor of the Kirk's committee on chaplains*.

Kirkcudbrightshire (pronounced *kir-coo-bree-sher* or *kir-coo-bree-shire*) Another name for **the Stewartry of Kirkcudbright**. See **stewartry**.

kirking or **kirkin** A **kirking** is a ceremonial attendance at a church, especially by councillors and officials after the election of a new town council: *At the traditional Kirking of the Council last month he averted a row over the robes by wearing a kilt in the McDuff tartan*.

kirk officer or **church officer** Another name for a **beadle**.

kirk session In a Presbyterian Church, the **kirk session** is the body responsible for governing the affairs of an individual church in a parish. It consists of the **minister** and the **elders**.

kist A **kist** is a large chest or wooden box. A **kist** is also the chest (the part of the body). The word is a Scottish form of *chest*.

kist o' whistles A **kist o' whistles** is a derogatory name for a church organ. The phrase, originally used by those opposed to the use of musical instruments in church, is now mainly literary. A **kist o' whistles** is also a wheezy chest or a person with a wheezy chest.

kittle or **kittlie** ① Someone who is **kittle** is unpredictable and capricious. To **kittle** also means to be puzzling or troubling to someone. ② Another sense of **kittle** is to tickle or be ticklish.

klondyker or **Klondyker** A **klondyker** is a large vessel which buys fish direct from the fishermen in Scottish waters, then processes the fish on board before returning to its home port, invariably in Eastern Europe: *Part of the Klondyker fleet, the vessel was reputedly bought by a Nigerian millionaire.* A **klondyker** can also be someone who works on one of these ships: *He said that the klondykers had remained relatively calm, despite the captain and most of the officers having been killed or injured by the blast.* The activity of buying and processing fish in this way is called

klondyking. The name comes from **Klondyke** in Alaska, a gold-mining centre, with allusion to the profits which could be made by fishermen who sold their fish to these factory ships.

knock Knock is an old-fashioned or literary word for a clock: *The old Tolbooth knock can still be seen in the town's museum.* **Knock** is a Scottish variant of *clock*.

knowe or **know** (pronounced *now*) A **knowe** is a small rounded hill. The word is a Scots form of *knoll*.

knype on (pronounced *knipe on*) To **knype on** is a Northeastern term meaning to keep going or slog away at something, often used in the sense of going steadily through life without any great mishap: *Aye knypin on?* It is sometimes shortened to **knype**: *"Foo ye doin?" "Oh, knypin."* **Knype** literally means to knock and is probably onomatopoeic in origin.

kye Kye are cattle. The word is a plural form of **coo**.

kyle A **kyle** is a narrow strait of the sea or narrow part of a river. It is used mainly in place names: *Kyle of Lochalsh; the Kyles of Bute.* The word comes from the Gaelic *caol* narrow.

laddie (rhymes with *daddy*) A **laddie** is a boy or young man: *He had the reputation of being a 'cheekie laddie', and hence of little use to the army.*

lade A **lade** is a watercourse, especially one that carries water to a mill. The latter is often called a **mill lade**: *The old mill lade off the River Leithen powered five woollen mills and a saw-mill.*

lad o' pairts (pronounced *lad-a-payrts*) A **lad o' pairts** is a youth, particularly one from a humble background, who is considered talented or promising: *This country prides itself on giving the lad o' pairts opportunities for advancement.*

laich or **laigh** (pronounced *layCH*) **Laich** means low: *a laich whisper.*

lair ① A **lair** is the ground for a grave in a cemetery, especially an area set aside for an individual or family. ② **Lair** can also mean mud or a muddy or boggy place. To **lair** is to sink in mud or in a bog: *The tractor had become laired in the mud.*

laird A **laird** is a lord, especially the owner of a large estate: *a sixteenth-century laird's mansion.*

laldie or **laldy** (pronounced *lal-dee*) To **gie it laldie**

means to do something vigorously: *Down one end of the room there was a gang of folkies giving it laldy, and good foot-tapping music filled the bar.*

Lallans (pronounced *lal-lanz*) **Lallans** is a name for the variety of Scots spoken in the Lowlands. It can also mean a literary version of this used by some twentieth-century Scottish writers. The word is a Scots version of *Lowlands*.

lament A **lament** is a slow traditional song or pipe tune composed in mourning for a death. It often features in titles of pieces of music: *MacCrimmon's Lament*; *Ossian's Lament*.

Lammas (pronounced *lam-us*) or **Lammas Day** One of the Scottish quarter days, **Lammas** falls on the first of August.

Lanarkshire (pronounced *lan-ark-sher* or *lan-ark-shire*) **Lanarkshire** is a former county of South Scotland which occupied much of the area on both sides of the River Clyde south and east of Glasgow. It is now administered by two single-tier local councils: North Lanarkshire and South Lanarkshire.

landward **Landward** means in, forming, or from the rural rather than urban parts of an area: *Edinburgh and the landward areas.*

lane A **lane** person or thing is lone or alone. **On one's lane** means on one's own, unaccompanied, or unaided: *She did it on her lane.*

lang Lang means long: *Yon's a lang road; Lang may your lum reek.*

lang-luggit (pronounced *lang-lug-it*) A **lang-luggit**, literally long-eared, person is someone who is inclined to eavesdrop.

Lang Toun The **Lang Toun** is a nickname for the town of Kirkcaldy.

laroch (pronounced *lar-oCH*) A **laroch** is the ruins or remains of a small domestic building such as a cottage. The word is originally from the Northeast, but is also used in literary Scots: *Only a few larochs show where the crofters' houses once stood.* It comes from the Gaelic *làrach* meaning a ruin.

lassie A **lassie** is a young girl: *She's a bonny wee lassie.*

laverock (pronounced *lav-er-ok* or *lave-rok*) A **laverock** is a skylark (the bird).

law ① In some areas of Scotland, particularly the Lowlands, a **law** is a hill, especially one which is rounded in shape. **Law** often forms part of the name of a hill, such as *Broad Law* or *Dundee Law*. ② **Law** can also mean low, as in *the Lawlands.*

lazy bed A **lazy bed** was, in former times, a patch of land in which potatoes were cultivated by laying them on the surface and covering them with manure or kelp and with soil from a trench on either side of the bed. Traces of them may still be seen particularly in now-unpopulated parts of the Highlands and Islands: *On the* *slope opposite the site of the township were hundreds of lazy-bed strips.*

lea' To **lea'** something or someone is to leave it or them.

leal (pronounced **leel**) To be **leal** is to be loyal or faithful. The term is literary or old-fashioned as is the use of the phrase **the land o' the leal** to mean heaven.

lea-rig Lea-rig is an old-fashioned term for a ridge of unploughed land.

lee To **lee** is to tell a lie or lies. A **lee** is a lie.

leet A **leet** is a list of candidates for a job, award, contract, etc. Sometimes an initial **long leet** of candidates is drawn up, and then whittled down to a final **short leet**: *She was on the short leet of four applicants interviewed on May 21.* The origin of the word is unclear: it is either from the Anglo-French *litte* a list, or from the same French source as *elite*.

left-footer (pronounced *left-foot-er*) or **left-fitter** In informal usage, a **left-footer** is a Roman Catholic. For the origin of this phrase see **kick**.

leid rhymes with (pronounced **deed**) A **leid** is a chiefly literary word for a language: *the auld Scots leid.* The term is Old English in origin.

len or **lend** A **len** is a loan: *Gie us a len o' a fiver.* To **take a len** of someone is to impose upon their good nature or gullibility.

let dab See **dab**.

lib To **lib** a farm animal is to castrate it.

libel In Scots Law a **libel** is the formal statement of a charge. To **libel** is to make such a statement: *I must plead guilty as libelled.*

licentiate A **licentiate** is a person holding a licence to preach, especially in the Presbyterian Church.

licht (pronounced *liCHt*) **Licht** means light.

lift The **lift** is a literary name for the sky. The word comes from the Old English *lyft*, and is related to the modern German *Luft*, which also means sky.

light The type of beer known as **light** is darker than **heavy** and less alcoholic. The nearest English equivalent is mild: *It's hard to find a place that sells a good pint of light these days.*

Light Blues One of the nicknames of Rangers football team is **the Light Blues**. They are probably so-called because their traditional shirts, while not particularly pale in colour, are lighter than those of Dundee, who are nicknamed *the Dark Blues.*

line The word **line** is used for any of various written notes or authorizations. A **sick line** or **doctor's line** is a sick note. A **bookie's line** is a betting slip. To **lift one's lines** is to formally withdraw one's membership from a particular Presbyterian church, especially when moving house.

links ① The word **links** means undulating sandy ground near a shore. It can also mean a golf course on such land: *a teasing 9-hole links; The hotel restaurant serves the kind of substantial Scottish/French cuisine you might need after a day on the links.* The word comes from the Old English *blincas*, the plural of *blinc* a ridge. ② Sausages in a string are also known as **links**.

linn A **linn** is a waterfall or the pool at the foot of one. A ravine or precipice may also be called a **linn**. The term comes from a combination of two words, the Gaelic *linne* a pool and the Old English *blynn* a torrent.

lintie (rhymes with *minty*) A **lintie** is a linnet: *singin like a lintie.*

Lion Rampant The **Lion Rampant** is a national emblem of Scotland, consisting of a red lion standing on its hind legs. A yellow flag with this design on it is also referred to as a **Lion Rampant**.

lippen To **lippen** is to trust or depend on: *Ye maunna lippen til him.*

loan or **loaning** A **loan** was originally a lane or path, especially one leading to a meadow, or a piece of uncultivated ground where cows were milked. The word is now most often found in the names of streets or places, such as *Grange Loan, Dobbie's Loan* and *Hoods Loaning.*

loch (pronounced *loCH*) A **loch** is a lake, as in *Loch Lomond* or *Loch Tay.* A long narrow bay or arm of the sea may also be called a **loch** or **sea loch**, as in *Loch Linnhe* or *Loch Fyne.* The word was originally Gaelic.

lochan (pronounced *loCH-an*) A **lochan** is a small lake: *The opposite bank of this elongated lochan is inaccessible to anglers.* The word comes from *loch* plus the Gaelic diminutive ending *-an*.

lockfast (pronounced *lock-fast*) When something, such as a premises, a door, or cupboard, is **lockfast** it is closed and secured by a lock. In Scots Law breaking into and stealing from a **lockfast** place is regarded as more serious than stealing from an unlocked place: *The housebreakers forced the lockfast cabinets and made off with five guns.*

Long Island The **Long Island** is a name used for the Outer Hebrides, or sometimes for Lewis and Harris only.

long lie A **long lie** is an occasion of staying in bed later than usual in the morning: *You look forward to a long lie on a Sunday.*

loon or **loun** In Northeast Scotland, a **loon** is a boy or lad: *He was a local loon, born and bred in Aberdeen.*

Lord Advocate The **Lord Advocate** is the chief law officer of the Crown in Scotland. He acts as public prosecutor and is in charge of the administration of criminal justice: *The trial ended when the charge was dropped by the Lord Advocate.*

Lord Justice-General The **Lord Justice-General** is the most senior criminal judge.

Lord President The **Lord President (of the Court of Session)** is the most senior civil judge. Nowadays the same person holds this office and that of **Lord Justice-General**.

Lord Provost Lord Provost is a title given to the **provost** of each of the cities of Edinburgh, Glasgow, Aberdeen, and Dundee.

Lorne sausage In the Glasgow area **Lorne sausage** is a name for sliced sausage meat.

loss To **loss** something is to lose it: *There's nae need tae loss the heid.*

Lothian (pronounced *loathe-ee-an*) **Lothian** is a former local government Region that occupied most of the area along the southern side of the Firth of Forth. It is now administered by four single-tier local councils: West Lothian, Midlothian, East Lothian, and the City of Edinburgh.

Lothians (pronounced *loathe-ee-anz*) The **Lothians** is a collective name for the former counties of East Lothian, West Lothian, and Midlothian, which lie on the south bank of the Firth of Forth: *the weather forecast for Edinburgh and the Lothians.*

loup or **lowp** (pronounced *lowp*) To **loup** is to leap or jump: *If you wait long enough, you might see a salmon louping.* A **loup** is a leap or jump. See also **loup the dyke** at **dyke**.

loupin or **lowpin** (pronounced *lowp-in*) ① In the Glasgow area **loupin** means throbbing or extremely sore: *Ma heid's loupin.* ② **Loupin** can also mean full of or infested by: *The pub was loupin wi football supporters.*

lowe (rhymes with *how*) A **lowe** is a flame or warm glow, such as that from a fire: *the lowe of the candle.* To **lowe** is to burn strongly but steadily: *There was aye a fire lowing in the grate.* The word is ultimately from the Old Norse *logi* a flame.

Lowland Lowland is used to refer to the Lowlands or to the dialects spoken there: *There was as an influx of Highlanders to Lowland towns in the late eighteenth century; Despite years of living abroad she has not lost her lowland accent.* A **Lowland** whisky is one distilled in the Lowlands.

Lowlands The word **Lowlands** is generally used to refer to any part of Scotland south or east of the Highlands. Sometimes, however, particularly in geographical contexts, it is used more specifically to refer to the low generally flat region of central Scotland, around the Forth and Clyde valleys, separating the Southern Uplands from the Highlands.

lowse (When an adjective, rhymes with *mouse*) When something is **lowse** it is loose. (When a verb, rhymes with *cows*) To **lowse** something is to loose or release it. To **lowse** can also mean to finish work: *They lowse at five o'clock.* **Lowsin time** is the time at which work or school finishes: *I'll get ye at the gate at lowsin time.*

low wines In whisky making, **low wines** is the name used for the weakly alcoholic product of the first distillation which is distilled a further time.

lucky bag A **lucky bag** is a sealed paper bag containing an unknown selection of sweets and cheap toys sold to children by confectioners.

lug A **lug** is an ear.

lum A **lum** is a chimney: *Run next door and tell them their lum's on fire!* The traditional saying **lang may your lum reek** (literally, long may your chimney smoke) is a way of wishing someone long life and prosperity.

lumber In the Glasgow area a **lumber** is a person one meets at a dance or party and with whom one establishes an amorous or sexual relationship: *You'll have no chance of getting a lumber if you go dressed like that.*

ma Ma means my: *It's ma first visit tae the islands.* See the entry for **my** for notes on the use of **ma** and **my** in Scots.

Mac- or **Mc-** Many Scottish (and Irish) surnames begin with **Mac-**, which is a Gaelic term meaning "son of-". For instance, *MacDonald* means "son of Donald", and *McInnes* is a Scots form of the Gaelic "MacAonghais", "son of Angus". Many surnames exist in both a **Mac-** and **Mc-** form, and the prefix may or may not be followed by a capital letter: *Sorley Maclean; John MacLean; Jim McLean.*

macallum (pronounced *ma-kal-um*) A **macallum** is vanilla ice-cream with raspberry juice or sauce on it, served in a dish. The term probably comes from the surname *Macallum*, although precisely why it came to be used of the ice-cream is unclear.

macer (rhymes with *racer*) The **macer** is the technical name in Scots Law for the official of a court whose duties include summoning witnesses to give evidence and keeping order in the court room. The equivalent in a court in England is the usher.

machair (pronounced *maCH-er*) Machair is a type of low-lying sandy grassy land found just above the high-water mark of many sandy shores in western Scotland, particularly in the Hebrides. It is often more fertile than the more mountainous areas further inland: *unspoilt miles of machair, beach and headland.* The word was originally Gaelic and meant a low-lying plain.

Machars (pronounced *maCH-erz*) The Machars is the area of Southwest Scotland occupying the fertile peninsula between Wigtown Bay and Luce Bay, two large inlets of the Solway Firth. It includes the Isle of Whithorn, site of the first Christian church in Scotland. The name comes from the Gaelic *machair* a low-lying plain.

Mackintosh A Mackintosh chair, building, etc. is one designed by the architect and artist **Charles Rennie Mackintosh** (1868-1928): *They also make dining tables in two Mackintosh designs.* His work was mainly Art Nouveau in style but has influences from traditional Scottish architecture and turn-of-the-century modernism. Among his major achievements are the design, both external and internal, of Glasgow School of Art and the Hill House in Helensburgh.

MacWhachle (pronounced *mac-whaCH-l*) In West Central Scotland, **wee MacWhachle** is a jocular nickname sometimes used for any toddler.

maindoor A **maindoor** flat is one which has its front door opening directly into the street or a garden rather than into a close or shared hallway: *a maindoor flat in Mayfield Road.*

Mainland The largest of the Shetland Islands and the largest of the Orkney Islands are both known as **Mainland**. A Shetlander or Orcadian would always mean this island when speaking of **the Mainland**, and would refer to the Scottish mainland as **Scotland**.

mains A **mains** is the home farm on an estate, cultivated by or for the landowner. The word is now generally only encountered in the names of farms: *Argrennan Mains; Mains of Cultmalundie.*

mair Mair means more: *Do ye want some mair?; Aye, that's mair like it.*

mairrit or **merrit** Mairrit means married: *Thirty-wan and you're no merrit yet?* To be **mairrit on** or **mairrit ontae** a person or family is to be married to that person or a member of that family: *He's mairrit ontae yin o the McDowells.*

maist Maist means most: *Maist o them arenae local.*

mak To mak something is to make it: *We thocht we'd better mak a start.*

makar (rhymes with *backer*) A **makar** is an old-fashioned or literary word for a poet, often used to refer to the major Scots poets of the 15th and early 16th century, such as Douglas, Dunbar, or Henryson.

malky (pronounced *malk-ee*) A **malky** is a Glasgow slang term for a razor used as a weapon. To **malky** someone is to slash them with a razor.

malt or **malt whisky** A **malt** is a whisky made in a **pot still** from dried germinated barley ("malt"). There are two types of malt whisky, the **single malt** which is the product of one distillery, and the **vatted malt** which is a blend of malt whiskies from various sources. If a whisky is a single malt, the label of the bottle will normally say so: *We have a range of malts to suit every mood and every occasion.*

mannie In some parts of Scotland, a **mannie** is any man: *the mannie from the gas board.* The plural is **mannies**. In the Northeast, the **mannie** is also the man in charge of something, especially if he is also its owner, for instance a farmer or the skipper of a fishing boat.

manse A **manse** is a house provided for a parish minister, and owned by the Church: *Kirk regulations dictate that a manse should have seven rooms.* Someone who is described as a **son** or **daughter of the manse** is the child of a minister. The word comes from the Medieval Latin *mansus* a dwelling, which is from the Latin *manēre* to remain.

mappie-mou (pronounced *map-ee-moo*) The **mappie-mou** is the name given in some parts of the Northeast to the antirrhinum or snapdragon. The term comes from *mappie*, a pet name for a rabbit, plus *mou* mouth.

Marches Riding of the Marches. See **Riding**.

Martinmas The 11th of November, **Martinmas**, is one of the four quarter-days or term-days in Scotland.

masel (pronounced *ma-sell*) **Masel** means myself: *Ah used tae play a bit masel.*

mask To **mask** tea is to make or brew it. When tea **masks** it is brewing or infusing. The word is related to *mash*.

Master The (male) heir of a Scottish viscount's or baron's title is known as the **Master** of the place the title is associated with: *the Master of Ballantrae*.

maun (pronounced *mawn*) **Maun** means must: *He maun hae dropped it.*

mavis A **mavis** is a song thrush. The name comes from the Old French *mauvis* a thrush.

maw ① **Maw** is a Central Scottish word for mother: *Away hame tae yer maw, ya big feartie!* ② In Orkney, Shetland, and the Far North, a seagull is known as a **maw**.

mawkit Something which is **mawkit** is very dirty: *a mawkit semmit*. **Mawkit** can also mean offensively bad: *That singing's mawkit!* Both senses of the word are most common in West Central Scotland. A *mauk* is an old Scots name for a maggot, and hence **mawkit** literally means putrid and infested with maggots.

mawsie (rhymes with *gauzy*) In the Northeast, a thick woollen garment, such as a jersey, is sometimes called a **mawsie**. The word may come from *marseille*, a type of heavy cotton fabric.

Mc- A variant of **Mac-**.

mealie pudding A **mealie pudding** is another name for a **white pudding**. It is so called because of the large amount of oatmeal it contains, oatmeal frequently being referred to in Scots simply as *meal*.

Mearns (pronounced *mernz*) **The Mearns** is an area of southern Northeast Scotland, occupying an area stretching inland from the coast between Stonehaven and the North Esk River north of Montrose, roughly equivalent to the old county of Kincardineshire.

meat Meat can be used not just to mean meat, but to mean any sort of food: *Rachel's no much of an eater, but the wee yin fair likes her meat.*

meen The **meen** is a Northeastern name for the moon.

meenit A **meenit** is a minute.

meggy-mony-feet (pronounced *meg-ee-mun-nee-feet*) In some areas, a centipede is known as a **meggy-mony-feet**.

meikle (rhymes with *treacle*) **Meikle** is one form of a Scots word meaning big or large. Nowadays it is mainly used in place names such as *Meikle Earnock*, and often distinguishes the larger of two neighbouring farms or estates with the same name, as in *Meikle Sypland* and *Little Sypland*. In everyday use, the form **muckle** is more common.

meiny (pronounced *mane-ee*) A **meiny** is a disparaging Northeastern word for a crowd or large group of people, a rabble. The word comes, via an earlier sense (a household or retinue), from the Old French *mesnie*, which in turn comes from the Latin *mansiō* a lodging.

melt To **melt** someone is to fell them with a blow or beat them up: *Shut it or I'll melt you!* This chiefly West

Central Scotland term comes from an older sense of **melt**, the spleen, and refers to the disabling effects of a hard blow over the spleen.

menage (pronounced *min-odge*) A **menage** is a savings club, for instance one run by employees at a place of work, which people pay a fixed sum of money into each week for a fixed period. The expression **couldnae run a menage** indicates that the organizational skills of the person being spoken about are not highly regarded: *A manager? Him? He couldnae run a menage!* The term comes from the French word *ménage*, one sense of which is housekeeping.

mercat (pronounced *mer-kit*) A **mercat** is a market.

mercat cross The **mercat cross** in a town is a monument in the form of a cross marking the site of the old market-place in a town.

-merchant Someone in West Central Scotland who is called a something-**merchant** is very fond of doing or consuming that thing. For example, a *patter-merchant* is someone who talks fluently and (they think) wittily in an effort to impress, and a *bevvy-merchant* is someone who regularly gets drunk.

merle (pronounced *merl*) The **merle** is a name, chiefly used in poetry, for the blackbird. The word comes via Old French from the Latin **merula**. *Merle* is also the modern French for blackbird.

merrit A variant of **mairrit**.

Merry Dancers The Aurora Borealis or Northern Lights, which are occasionally visible from Northern Scotland, are sometimes called **the Merry Dancers**.

merse (rhymes with *verse*) In Southern Scotland, an area of low-lying fertile land near a river or shore is known as a **merse**. **The Merse** is a low-lying fertile region in the Eastern Borders, between the River Tweed and the Lammermuir Hills. The word comes from Old English, where it meant marsh.

messages The **messages** are the everyday shopping, especially groceries, for a household: *I'll get the messages on my way back from work; She put the bag of messages on the table.* To **go the messages** or **do the messages** is to do everyday household shopping: *I have to go the messages for my grannie every time I visit her.* The term comes from the sense of *message* meaning a mission or errand, which was extended to cover the things bought on the errand.

messan (pronounced *mess-an*) A **messan** is a Central and Southern name for an obnoxious or contemptible person: *Stop that right now, ye dirty wee messan!* An earlier sense of **messan** was a dog, either a mongrel or a lap-dog, which comes from the Gaelic *measan* meaning small pet dog.

micht (pronounced *miCHt*) **Micht** means might (in all its senses): *Ah weel, ye micht be richt.*

michty me **Michty me!** is a mild oath.

mickle In the proverb **mony a mickle maks a muckle**, a **mickle** is a small amount. This is the exact opposite of the original meaning, since **mickle** was originally a variant of **muckle**, a large amount.

midden In urban Central Scotland, the **midden** is the area at the back of a block of flats where the communal dustbins are kept. In rural parts, a **midden** is a dunghill. Throughout Scotland, **midden** is used to describe any dirty or untidy person or thing: *Are you ever going to clean this place up, ye dirty auld midden?*; *This room's a right midden.*

midgie ① A **midgie** is a midge. ② In some areas, a **midgie** or **midgie-bin** is a name for a dustbin or litter bin. A **midgie man**, therefore, is a refuse collector. A **midgie raker**, on the other hand, is a tramp who hunts through litter bins for objects they think are useful or valuable. **Midgie** is a variant of **midden**.

Midlothian Midlothian is the area of East Central Scotland immediately southeast of Edinburgh. The former county with this name included the city of Edinburgh as well. **Midlothian** is now a single-tier local council administering the area southeast of Edinburgh but not the city itself.

miller To **drown the miller** is to dilute a drink such as whisky or tea with too much water.

mince Despite the popularity of **mince** as a foodstuff, in the Glasgow area the word has entered the language as a term for rubbish or nonsense: *I got dead nervous and sat there talking absolute mince*; *You'll get no sense from him. His brain's mince.* Someone who is **as thick as mince** is exceptionally stupid. To **sicken someone's mince** is to spoil a successful-looking situation for them, to knock the wind out of their sails.

Minch (pronounced *minsh*) or **the Minches** The **Minch** is a channel of the Atlantic divided into the **North Minch**, between the Scottish mainland and the Isle of Lewis, and the **Little Minch**, between the Isle of Skye and Harris and North Uist.

mind To **mind** something is to remember it: *Ah mind when it was a' green fields here.* If something **minds** you of something, it reminds you of it or causes you to remember it: *That minds me o the time Wullie tried tae get aff wi that French lassie.*

minding A **minding** is a small gift given as a token of goodwill.

mines Mines is a broad Scots form of mine: *That wan's mines!*

ming To **ming** is to smell strongly and unpleasantly: *My clothes always end up minging of stale cigarette smoke when I go to the pub.* A **ming** is a strong unpleasant smell or stink.

mingin (pronounced *ming-in*) Something which is **mingin** smells strongly and unpleasantly. To be **mingin** is also to be very unpleasant or of very poor quality: *The weather's been mingin aw week.*

minister A **minister** is a man or woman who is a member of the Clergy in the church of Scotland or another Presbyterian Church: *The local Church of Scotland minister confirmed that the hall had been advertised for sale; My grandfather was a minister. in Orkney.*

miraculous (pronounced *mir-rock-you-luss*) To be **miraculous** is to be exceptionally drunk.

miserable Someone who is **miserable** is mean or stingy: *Ye'll no get much of a donation from him: he's as miserable as the rest of his family.*

missives In buying or selling a house or flat, the **missives** are formal letters exchanged between the buyer's and seller's solicitors which commit both parties to the deal at the price and on the conditions stated in the letters.

miss oneself To **miss oneself** is to be deprived of pleasure through not being present at an enjoyable or entertaining occasion: *You really missed yourself last night. We'd a great time.*

mither (rhymes with *dither*) **Mither** means mother: *Aye, lad, ye'll be a man afore your mither; the mither tongue.*

mixter-maxter (pronounced *mix-ter-max-ter*) or **mixtie-maxtie** **Mixter-maxter** means in an untidy jumbled way or state: *Papers were strewn mixter-maxter across the desk.* A **mixter-maxter** is a confused jumble: *The film contains a mixter-maxter of inadequately thought out ideas.*

mochie or **mochy** (pronounced *moCH-ee*) **Mochie** is a word used in some areas to describe damp, misty, and unpleasantly humid weather or air. The word is from the Old Norse *mugga* mist.

Mod The **Mod** is an annual festival of Gaelic language and culture, in which prizes are given for singing, dancing, etc. It is held in a different town each year, usually in the Highlands but sometimes in a Lowland or overseas town with a large community of Highland origin. The name comes from the Gaelic *mōd* assembly.

moderator A **moderator** is a person chosen to chair a meeting, particularly in a presbyterian Church. **The Moderator** is a minister in the Church of Scotland who is elected for a period of one year to chair meetings of the Kirk's **General Assembly** and to act as the Church's representative on various formal occasions: *the Moderator of the General Assembly of the Church of Scotland*. The word comes from the French **modérateur**, the president of a Protestant Assembly.

mollach (pronounced *moll-aCH*) To **mollach** about is a Northeastern term meaning to hang around or wander about aimlessly: *Fit are ye mollachin aboot at?* The expression comes from *mole* the animal, plus the diminutive ending *-ach*, presumably alluding to the seemingly random way molehills pop up in a field or garden.

mony (pronounced *mun-nee* or *mon-nee*) **Mony** means many: *There's no mony jobs left round here.*

moo or **mou** The **moo** is the mouth.

moose A **moose** is a mouse.

mooth The **mooth** is the mouth.

moothie (rhymes with *toothy*) A **moothie** is a mouth-organ or harmonica: *He's one of the best moothie players in all Scotland.*

Moray (pronounced _mur-ree_) **Moray** is an area and former county in Northeast Scotland, occupying part of the coastal area between Inverness and Fraserburgh. It is now the name of a single-tier local council administering much the same area as the old county. The **Moray Firth** is an inlet of the North Sea between the Northeastern coast and the coast of Ross and Cromarty.

morn In much of Scotland, people refer to tomorrow as **the morn**: _Any chance of a lift to Dumfries the morn?_ **The morn's morn** is tomorrow morning, and **the morn's nicht** is tomorrow night.

Morningside A **Morningside** accent is the Edinburgh name for a widely mocked upper-middle class Scottish accent, named after a prosperous residential area of south Edinburgh. One of its characteristics is the pronunciation of "ah" as "eh", which has given rise to the jibe that people in Morningside think that "sex" is what coal is delivered in, and that a "creche" is a road accident. In Glasgow the equivalent accent is known as **Kelvinside**. **Morningside** is also used in allusion to the prim, genteel and conservative attitudes traditionally attributed to upper-middle class people in Edinburgh: _like a Morningside matriarch disgustedly twitching her curtains at the soiled laundry on her neighbour's line._

morra The **morra** is a broad Glasgow term for tomorrow: _Should be a cracking gemme the morra._

mou A variant spelling of **moo**.

mouth music Mouth music is a form of singing using no words, or a very few simple and repetitive words, to sing tunes which were originally written as instrumental music. The term is a translation of the Gaelic *port a beul*, music from mouth.

mowdie (rhymes with *rowdy*) or **mowdiewart** (pronounced *mowd-ee-wort*) A **mowdie** is a mole (the animal). The word comes from *moldewarpe*, literally meaning earth-thrower, an archaic name for a mole.

muckle Something which is **muckle** is large: *a muckle great hole*. **Muckle** can also be used figuratively to suggest that something is an extreme example of its kind: *Ye muckle sumph!* **Muckle** also means much: *You'll no get muckle sense fae him.* In place names, the variant **meikle** is often used instead.

muir (pronounced *myoor*) A **muir** is a moor. The word often forms part of place names, as in *Muir of Ord*, *Muirhouse*, or *Kirriemuir*.

mull A **mull** is a headland or narrow peninsula. The word is mainly encountered in place names such as the *Mull of Kintyre* or the *Mull of Galloway*. The word comes from the Gaelic *maol* a headland.

Mulleachd (pronounced *mull-yaCH*) A **Mulleachd** is a person from Mull, especially one who was brought up on the island.

Munro (pronounced *mun-roe*) A **Munro** is any of the 284 Scottish mountain peaks over 3 000 feet (approx 915 metres) in height: *It's a pretty impressive feat to climb that* *many Munros.* Compare the smaller **Corbett** and **Donald**. They are named after Hugh Thomas *Munro* (1856-1919), who published a list of them in 1891.

Munro-bagger A **Munro-bagger** is a term for someone who is attempting to climb every mountain in Scotland more than 3 000 ft high. Among hillwalkers and mountaineers it is often used derogatorily with the implication that, by concentrating purely on the size of a hill, the Munro-bagger is missing the true point of the activity. Someone who is trying to climb every Munro is said to be **Munro-bagging**.

murder polis! (pronounced *po-liss*) **Murder polis!** is a frequently jocular cry for help in any confused or awkward situation, used mainly in the Glasgow area. If a situation is described as **murder polis** it is very confused and noisy: *It's always murder polis in the shops before Christmas.*

my Scots frequently uses **my** and other possessive pronouns in situations where English either omits them or uses a word like "some" instead: *I'm away home for my tea; I got it for my Christmas; Away up the stair to your bed, you.*

-na or **-nae** The suffix **-na** when added to a verb forms the negative, as in *dinna* or *cannae*: *Dinna dae that; I cannae mind his name; He hasnae got the hang o it.*

nabbler A **nabbler** is a Northeastern word for a fast and skilful worker.

nae (pronounced *nay*) **Nae** means no or not: *There's nae mair; She'll nae be back yet.*

Nairn **Nairn** or **Nairnshire** is a former county in the North of Scotland, at the western end of the Moray Firth east of Inverness. It is now administered by Highland single-tier local council.

nane **Nane** means none: *There was nane left.*

nash In the Edinburgh area to **nash** is to hurry or dash: *I'll just nash along to the shop for a paper.*

natural philosophy In the ancient Scottish universities **natural philosophy** is the name used for physics: *the Natural Philosophy lecture theatre.*

neb A **neb** is a nose, beak, or projecting point.

nebby or **nebbie** A **nebby** person is nosey or inquisitive. **Nebby** can also mean sharp-tongued or cheeky: *You nebby wee besom!*

neck When a bottle of beer is served **by the neck** it is not poured into a glass: *Two bottles of lager by the neck please.*

ned In the Glasgow area a **ned** is a young hooligan or petty criminal: *He's a right wee ned.*

neebur (pronounced *neeb-er*) A **neebur** is a neighbour.

neep A **neep** is a turnip: *haggis and neeps.*

Ne'erday (pronounced *nayr-day*) **Ne'erday** is New Year's Day: *the Ne'erday television highlights.*

Nessie The legendary aquatic monster of Loch Ness is familiarly known as **Nessie**.

neuk (pronounced *nyook*) A **neuk** is a corner or nook. It may also mean an area of land that projects into the sea, as in the *East Neuk of Fife.*

nicht (pronounced *niCHt*) **Nicht** means night. **The nicht** means tonight: *We'll no go far the nicht.*

nicky-tams (pronounced *nick-ee-tamz*) **Nicky-tams** are straps or strings secured round trouser legs below the knee, formerly worn especially by farm workers to keep the trouser bottoms clear of dirt.

nineteen-canteen (pronounced *nine-teen-can-teen*) In the Glasgow area **nineteen-canteen** means any undefined time in the distant past: *He's had that motor since nineteen-canteen.*

nip To **nip someone's heid** is to irritate someone by constant nagging: *Ah had to get oot the hoose. She'd been nippin ma heid all day.* To **nip** a cigarette is a Glasgow term meaning to put it out before it is finished, usually with the intention of finishing it later. A **nip** is a partly-smoked extinguished cigarette.

nippy sweetie In the Glasgow area an irritable sharp-tongued person may be described as a **nippy sweetie**. The term is an extended use of the original meaning, which was a sweet with a relatively sharp or tart flavour.

no No means not: *He's no weel.*

nocht (pronounced *noCHt*) Nocht means nothing: *It's nocht tae dae wi you.* The word is a Scots form of *nought*.

noo Noo means now: *Whit's wrang noo?* **The noo** or the **now** means just now, at this exact moment: *Hurry up, we're gaun the noo.*

nor Nor is sometimes used to mean than: *She's got mair nor me.*

Northern Isles The Orkneys, Shetlands, and Fair Isle are known collectively as the **Northern Isles**.

not proven (rhymes with *woven*) In Scots Law **not proven** is a third verdict available in court, returned when there is evidence against the defendant but insufficient to convict. In the case of such a verdict the defendant is unconditionally discharged.

nowt (rhymes with *shout*) In some parts of Scotland a **nowt** is a bullock. **Nowt** can also be a plural word for cattle.

numpty In the Glasgow area a **numpty** is a stupid person: *That's no the way to do it, ya numpty!*

nyaff (pronounced *nyaff*) A **nyaff** is a worthless person, particularly a small one: *Never mind what that wee nyaff says.* The word is perhaps an imitation of the barking of a small dog.

o O means of: *Three pun o tatties, please; Whit d'ye make o that?*

oatcake An **oatcake** is a thin unsweetened oatmeal biscuit, an example of the importance of oats in the traditional Scottish diet which gave rise to Samuel Johnson's cheeky definition of oats as "A grain, which in England is generally given to horses, but in Scotland supports the people": *Scottish farmhouse cheeses accompanied by oatcakes and wholemeal crackers.*

obligement An **obligement** is a kind, helpful act or favour: *Could you do me a wee obligement?*

och (pronounced *oCH*) **Och** is an expression of surprise, contempt, annoyance, impatience, or disagreement: *Och, away ye go!* It is also used as a general preface to any remark: *Och, I think I'll away to my bed.*

ochone (pronounced *oCH-own*) **Ochone** is an expression of sorrow or regret. It is now old-fashioned and more likely to be found in stage or caricature representations of Highland English: *Ochone, ochone, whatever will come of it?* The word was originally Gaelic.

ocht (pronounced *oCHt*) **Ocht** means anything: *Ah dinnae ken ocht aboot it.* The term is a Scots form of **aught**.

offie (rhymes with *coffee*) In the Glasgow area an **offie** is an off-licence: *We'll need to get a carry-out before the offies shut.*

offski Offski is a Glaswegian slang term meaning leaving, on one's way: *Right, that's me offski.*

O Grade O Grade or **Ordinary Grade** was until recently the basic level of the Scottish Certificate of Education, now largely replaced by the **Standard Grade**: *O grade Geography.* It is also used to mean a pass in a particular subject: *She has ten O grades.*

old-fashioned A child who is described as **old-fashioned** is regarded as old for their age or precocious.

Old Firm The Old Firm is a term used to mean Celtic and Rangers, the two main Glasgow football teams, conceived as together forming a footballing establishment: *next Saturday's Old Firm League meeting; the Old Firm's stranglehold on Scottish football.*

ongoings Ongoings are happenings or events; goings-on.

ony (rhymes with *pony*) Ony means any: *Is there ony mair?*

oor Oor means our: *oor national gemme.*

oose (pronounced *ooss*) Oose is dust or fluff: *Have you seen the oose under that bed?* Something dusty or covered in fluff may be described as **oosy**. Oose was originally the plural of *oo*, a Scots word for wool.

oot Oot means out: *Are ye gaun oot the night?*

Orange The term **Orange** is applied to anything or anyone connected with the Orangemen, a society dedicated to upholding the Protestant religion, the Protestant dynasty, and Protestant supremacy against Irish Nationalists and Roman Catholics: *the Orange Hall*. They are organized in **Orange Lodges**. An **Orange Walk** is a march by Orangemen, especially occurring in West Central Scotland. The main one is held on the Saturday nearest to the twelfth of July (the anniversary of the Battle of the Boyne). The term refers to William of *Orange*, who as King William the Third, successfully resisted attempts to restore the Catholic Stuart dynasty.

Orcadian (pronounced *or-kay-dee-an*) An **Orcadian** is a native or inhabitant of the Orkneys. The word comes from the Latin *Orcades* Orkneys.

Ordinary Degree In older Scottish Universities an **Ordinary Degree** is a degree gained by students studying courses at a lower (Ordinary) level, as opposed to courses at an Honours level.

Ordinary grade Ordinary grade is the full form of O grade.

Orkney Orkney, also known as **the Orkneys** or **the Orkney Islands**, is a group of over 70 islands which lies off the North coast of Scotland and is separated from the Scottish mainland by the Pentland Firth. The islands are predominantly low-lying and treeless.

orra (pronounced *or-ra* or *or-ree*) In Tayside and the Northeast, **orra** means coarse or uncouth in behaviour

or speech: *When she talks like that we feel all orra and common.*
On a traditional Scottish farm, an **orraman**, **orra lad** or,
(in the Northeast) **orra loon** was a man or boy
employed to do miscellaneous unskilled work. Earlier
senses of the word meant odd or occasional, and it
perhaps comes from *ower a'* over all, everywhere or
general.

outby (pronounced *out-by*) or **ootby** (pronounced *oot-by*) Outby means outlying, away from a specific place
such as a house, a town, a farm, or a shore: *the outby fields.*
It can also mean outside, not in the house: *ootby in the
summer sunshine.*

outsider In the Glasgow area an **outsider** is the first or
last slice from a loaf of bread.

outwith (pronounced *out-with*) Outwith means outside
or beyond: *parts of Edinburgh outwith the city centre; Alcohol
would not be served outwith existing licensing hours.*

ower (rhymes with *power*) Ower means over: *He flung it
ower the wa.* It also means over in the sense of too or
excessively: *It's ower warm for a jumper.*

owergyaan (pronounced *our-gyahn*) or **owergan**
(pronounced *our-gan*) An **owergyaan** is a Northeastern
word meaning a scolding or telling-off. Compare the
English *going-over*, a scolding or thrashing.

oxter An **oxter** is an armpit.

Paddy's Market In parts of West Central Scotland, an untidy or confused place or situation is sometimes described as being like **Paddy's Market**: *It's like Paddy's Market in here.* The term comes from the name of a Glasgow flea market popular with the city's Irish population in the late 19th century (and still going today).

Paddy's Milestone Ailsa Craig, a high rocky island in the Firth of Clyde off the coast from Girvan, is jocularly known as **Paddy's Milestone** because it is a prominent landmark on the sea route from Ireland to Glasgow.

pair A variant of **puir** (poor).

pairt A **pairt** is a part: *people in foreign pairts.* To **pairt** is to part. See also **lad o' pairts**.

paisley pattern A **paisley pattern** is a type of pattern of small curving shapes with intricate detailing, usually printed or woven in bright colours, which although originally of Kashmiri design was associated with the town of Paisley in Renfrewshire where much material with such a pattern was made. Something made of material with this pattern on it can be described either as **paisley-pattern** or simply as **paisley**: *a paisley-pattern tie; a paisley shawl.*

Paisley screwdriver or **Glesca screwdriver** A **Paisley screwdriver** is a jocular Glaswegian term for a hammer. In some other areas, the term **Glesca screwdriver** is used instead. Both versions of the phrase allude to the alleged stupidity of people in the specified town.

paldies (pronounced *paul-deez*) A variant spelling of **pauldies**.

pan In a Scottish kitchen, a cooking vessel with a long handle on one side of it is generally referred to as a **pan** rather than a pot. To **knock one's pan in** is to tire oneself out through hard work: *I've been knocking my pan in all day — can ye no let me have a minute's peace?*

pancake A **pancake** is a round flat cake cooked on a griddle, smaller and thicker than an English pancake and usually eaten cold with jam, butter, etc. In England it is known as a drop scone or a Scotch pancake.

pan drop A **pan drop** is a type of hard round white mint sweet with a rounded top and bottom and a hard centre. It is also known as a mint imperial.

panel In Scots Law, the **panel** is the accused person in the dock during a criminal trial.

pan loaf A **pan loaf** is a loaf of bread with a light crust all round, rather than just on the top and bottom.

Pan bread is bread from such a loaf. They are so called because each loaf was baked in an individual baking tin or pan. Compare **plain loaf**. A **pan-loaf** voice or accent is a posh one. This idiom has developed because pan loaves were originally dearer than plain ones.

pap ① To **pap** something is to throw it: *Pap that in the bucket, will you?* To be **papped out** of a place is to be forced to leave it: *He got papped out of the Uni after failing his resits.* ② A **pap** is a female breast. The word is also used in the name of various conical, roughly breast-shaped, hills: *the Paps of Jura; Maiden Pap.*

Pape A Pape is an offensive and derogatory name for a Roman Catholic, used mainly in West Central Scotland: *an obnoxious bigot who hadn't spoken to his own sister ever since she married "that Pape".* The word is a shortening of **papist**.

Paradise Celtic Football Club's stadium in the Parkhead area of Glasgow is nicknamed **Paradise** by Celtic fans. The nickname apparently refers to the high quality of the facilities when the stadium opened in 1892.

paraphrase In the Church of Scotland and other Presbyterian churches, a **paraphrase** is a passage from the Bible that has been set in verse so that it can be sung.

park A **park** on a farm is an enclosed field, whether for growing crops or grazing animals: *I steered the beasts down to the park beside the main road; the hay parks.* The playing area of a football, rugby, or shinty ground is sometimes called **the park**: a usage which has spread from Scotland to the rest of Britain: *Ever wondered what physios have in those huge bags which they lug on to the park to treat injured players?*

parritch Parritch is an old-fashioned word for porridge. See also **auld claes and parritch** at **claes**.

Pars Dunfermline football team is nicknamed **the Pars**: *The Pars look set to extend their unbeaten run to five games.*

partan (pronounced *part-an*) A **partan** is a crab, especially a common edible crab. **Partan bree** is a type of crab soup. The word comes from Gaelic.

patent still A **patent still** is a type of still used in producing grain whisky, which is capable of operating continuously. It consists of two tall linked cylindrical tanks, in the first of which the **wash** (a liquid rather like weak beer) is broken down into its component parts, which are selectively condensed in the second tank so that the impurities, which condense at a different temperature from the liquid which will become the whisky, can be removed. Compare **pot still**.

pauchle (pronounced *pawCH-l*) A variant spelling of **pochle**.

pauldies or **paldies** (pronounced *paul-deez*) In some areas of Eastern Scotland, the game of hopscotch is known as **pauldies**. The stone used in this game is sometimes known as a **pauldie**. See also **beds** and **peever**. The name comes from the French word *palet*, a stone thrown at a target in some games.

paw Paw is a word for father used in Central Scotland: *maw, paw and the weans.*

pawkie or **pawky** Someone or something which is **pawkie** has or shows a dry sense of humour which includes a shrewd and down-to-earth criticism of hypocrisy or pretension: *learned enthusiasm sprinkled with a pawky sense of humour.* The word comes from the old noun *pawk* a trick.

peace To **be, sit** or **lie at peace** is to remain still: *The weans won't sit at peace for a moment.* To **give someone peace** is to be quiet and leave them alone: it is most frequently heard as a request or command: *Ah'll do it later, Ah said. Just gie me peace till Ah've had ma tea, okay?*

peasebrose (pronounced *peas-broze*) Peasebrose is an old-fashioned dish made by stirring boiling water into flour made from dried ground peas.

pech (pronounced *peCH*) To **pech** is to pant for breath, especially because of effort or exertion: *We were all peching by the time we reached the top.* To be **peched out** is to be exhausted and out of breath.

Peeblesshire (pronounced *pee-blz-sher* or *pee-blz-shire*) Peeblesshire is a former inland county of Southeast Scotland. It is now administered by Borders single-tier local council.

peedie An Orkney and Caithness variant of **peerie** (in the sense: small or wee).

peel or **peel tower** A **peel** is a type of fortified tower house dating from the 16th century found on both sides of the border between Scotland and England: *a converted peel tower near Selkirk.* The word comes, via an obsolete sense meaning a fence made of stakes, from the Old French *piel* a stake. It is related to *pale* (in the sense: a stake or boundary) and *paling*.

peely-wally or **peelie-wallie** (pronounced *peel-ee-wal-lee*) Someone who is **peely-wally** is pale and unhealthy-looking. To feel **peely-wally** is to feel slightly unwell. Something which is **peely-wally** is lacking in the strength or vigour thought desirable: *This tea's a bit peely-wally; The team's peely-wally performance frustrated the fans.* The origin of the term is not entirely clear: it probably comes from the earlier *peelie* or *palie* meaning pale, sickly or feeble-looking, but might also be influenced by *wallie* meaning china or porcelain, with a reference to its pale colour.

peen A **peen** is a pin.

peenge To **peenge** is to moan or complain in a whining, peevish manner: *Stop peenging, we've only got a little further to go.*

peeny or **peenie** A **peeny** is an apron. In Central Scotland, the **peeny** is also a child's word for the stomach: *a pain in the peeny.* It was originally a child's word for *pinafore*.

peep A **peep** is the lowest level at which a gas flame can be put without going out. To **put someone's gas at a peep** is to put them in their place or knock the wind out of their sails: *The ban on taping trials puts the cassette-carrying reporters' gas at a peep.*

peerie ① A **peerie** is a child's spinning top. This sense of the word probably comes from *peir*, an old Scots word for a pear, alluding to the top's shape. ② **Peerie** or **peedie** means small or wee: *a peerie back room; his peedie brither.* **Peerie** is the form found in Shetland, **peedie** in Caithness, and the two forms co-exist in Orkney. Its origin is unclear, although it may be related to the Norwegian dialect *piren* meaning niggardly or thin.

peerie heels In Central and Southern Scotland, stiletto heels are sometimes called **peerie heels**.

peever The game of hopscotch is known as **peever** or **peevers** in some parts of Central and Southern Scotland. The flat stone etc. used in this game is also known as a **peever**. See also **beds** and **pauldies**.

peewit (pronounced *pee-wit*), **peesweep** (pronounced *peez-weep*) or **peesie** (pronounced *peas-ee*) The **peewit** is the standard Scottish name, (also used in parts of England), for the lapwing, a type of plover common on shores and grasslands throughout Britain. **Peesweep** and **peesie** are Scottish dialect forms. The name is imitative of the bird's cry.

pend A **pend** is an arched passageway at the entrance to a lane or courtyard: *Access to the site is through a pend in Cochrane Street.* The word ultimately comes from the Latin *pendēre* to hang.

perjink (pronounced *per-jink*) Someone who is **perjink**

is neat and precise about things to the point of being fussy or prim: *She's awful perjink about her appearance.*

Perthshire (pronounced *perth-sher* or *perth-shire*) **Perthshire** is a former inland county in central Scotland. It is now administered by two single-tier local councils: Perthshire & Kinross and Stirling.

petted lip If a child has a **petted lip**, its lower lip is stuck out in a sulk.

pibroch (pronounced *pea-broCH*) A **pibroch** is a piece of music for the bagpipes, consisting of a theme known as the **ground** or **ùrlar** followed by a set of variations which make increasingly elaborate use of grace notes and other ornamentation. **Pibroch**, also known as **ceol mor**, is also the name given to such pieces collectively. The word is a Scots form of the Gaelic *piobaireachd*, piping or pipe-music, which comes from *piobair*, a piper.

pickle or **puckle** A **pickle** is an indeterminate but fairly small amount or number of something. When speaking about a **pickle** of something, the word "of" is often omitted: *a pickle snow.* Sometimes, through the Scots fondness for understatement, a **pickle** comes to mean a lot rather than a little: *A thirty-inch pipe? There'll be a pickle gas in that.*

Pict A **Pict** was a member of the people who lived in Scotland north of the Forth and Clyde in the first to fourth centuries A.D: *The area became the last refuge of the Picts when the Scots invaded from Ireland.* Something which is **Pictish** is associated with or created by the Picts: *a Pictish* *stone carving.* The word comes from the Late Latin *Pictī* painted men.

pie In Scotland, unless some other variety is specified, the word **pie** refers to a small round pie made of hot-water pastry and filled with minced mutton. It is sometimes known as a **mutton pie** or a **Scotch pie**: *pie, beans, and chips.*

piece A **piece** is a sandwich or slice of bread eaten as part of a packed lunch or as a snack: *a jeely piece; a piece and cheese.*

piece box A **piece box** is a box used for carrying sandwiches or a snack to work or school: *I opened my bag and took out my piece box and flask.*

piler A **piler** is the name given in some areas to a child's homemade vehicle constructed from pram wheels, wooden boxes, etc. Elsewhere this is known as a **bogie**, **cairtie**, **geggie** or **hurlie**. The term comes from the verb *pile* meaning to swing or push with one's legs so as to increase the speed of a swing, scooter, etc.

pinkie The **pinkie** is the little finger. In Northeast Scotland the word **crannie** is used instead. The word comes from the Dutch *pink* the little finger.

pipe Pipe music is music for the bagpipes: *a pipe tune which is believed to be over 500 years old.* A **pipe band** is a band consisting of a number of bagpipers and drummers: *Irvine Pipe Band.*

piper A **piper** is a bagpipes player: *A solo piper opens Aberdeen Highland Games at 10am on Sunday.*

pipes The **pipes** can mean either a set of bagpipes or a group of bagpipe players: *a lament played on the pipes; the pipes and drums of the Royal Scots Dragoon Guards.*

pirn A **pirn** is a reel or bobbin for holding thread: *Traditional hand-weaving required one person to work the loom, and another to wind the pirns.*

pish Pish is the usual Scots word for piss: *Ah'm away for a pish; It was pishing down outside.* Someone who is **pished** is drunk. Something which is **pish** is of very poor quality: *Okay, it was a pish programme, but we enjoyed appearing on it.*

Piskie A **Piskie** is a member of the Scottish Episcopal Church: *the effort made by Piskies like myself to explain that we were not "the English Church".* Something which is described as **Piskie** is associated with, or typical of, the Episcopal Church: *a typical Piskie service.* The word is a contraction of *Episcopal.*

pit Pit means put: *Where did he pit it?* The past tense can be either **pit** or **put**, and the past participle can be either **pit** or **pitten**.

plaid (rhymes with *laid*) A **plaid** is a long piece of tartan cloth worn over one shoulder as part of Highland costume, nowadays mainly seen as part of the formal dress of military pipers. The word comes from the Gaelic *plaide*, and is perhaps connected to the English word *ply* to twist or fold together.

plain loaf A **plain loaf** is a loaf with a crisp crust at the top and bottom, but none at the sides or ends. **Plain bread** is bread from such a loaf. Compare **pan loaf**.

plank To **plank** something, or **plank it away**, is to put it away somewhere safe or hidden for later use: *The old man's got a few cans planked away somewhere.* To **plank** something somewhere is to place or put it there in a forceful manner: *He planked the file down on the desk in front of me.* A **plank** is a secret supply or cache of something.

play oneself To **play oneself** is to waste time, mess about, or do something half-heartedly rather than work properly at it: *Are you going to help us with this, or are you just going to sit there playing yourself all day?*

playpiece A **playpiece** is something, such as a biscuit, a packet of crisps, or an apple, that a child takes to school to eat during the morning break or interval.

pled In Scotland, and particularly in legal contexts, **pled** is used instead of "pleaded" as the past of plead: *He pled guilty to three charges of theft.*

plettie Plettie is a Dundonian term for a balcony or landing in a block of flats. The word comes from *plat* meaning flat or level, which is ultimately from the same source as *plate* and *platform.*

plook or **plouk** A **plook** is a pimple. Someone who is **plooky** or **plookit** has a lot of pimples. The word probably comes from Middle English *plowke.* It is connected with the Gaelic words *pluc* a lump or heap and *plucan* a pimple, but it is more likely that the Gaelic is derived from the Scots than vice-versa.

plot To **plot** is a chiefly Northeastern word meaning to sweat. To **plot** a hen or chicken is to scald its carcass with boiling water to make it easier to pluck. The word probably comes from the Middle Dutch *ploten*, to strip the wool from a fleece by dipping it in a hot chemical solution.

plouter (rhymes with *doubter*) To **plouter** is to splash through, or play about with, water or mud. To **plouter** or **plouter about** is to do something in an aimless manner, to potter or fiddle about. The word probably comes from the Scots *plowt*, an onomatopoeic word for a heavy fall or loud splash, but it may be related to the Dutch *ploeteren* to splash or dabble.

plump A **plump** is a sudden, heavy fall of rain: *A heavy plump of rain sent them scurrying for shelter.*

plunk To **plunk** school or a class is to play truant from it: *She plunked classes one afternoon to take part in a talent contest.* The word is used in parts of Central and Southern Scotland.

pochle (pronounced *poCH-l*) or **pauchle** To **pochle** something, for example a vote or figure, is to dishonestly rig or fix it so that a particular result is obtained: *He is widely believed to be the man who pochled the votes; To some people it is "creative accountancy", to others it is simply pochling the books.* A **pochle** is an instance of cheating; a swindle or fiddle: *The chairman's wife won first prize in the raffle: talk about a pochle!* In some areas, something a person takes home from work, either as a legitimate perk or through theft, is also known as a **pochle**. The word comes from the Old Scots *pakkald*, and is ultimately derived from *pack* a bundle.

poind (pronounced *pinned*) To **poind** is the Scots Law term meaning to value and forbid the sale of the property of a debtor so that it can be sold in a **warrant sale**, the proceeds of which are put towards the repayment of the debt. The act of doing this is known as a **poinding**: *a poinding of household goods for non-payment of poll tax.* The word is a variant of the Old English *pyndan* to impound.

poke A **poke** is a bag, especially a small paper one: *a poke of chips.* The word comes from the Old Northern French *poque* and is also used in the North of England.

pokey-hat A **pokey-hat** is a Central Scottish word for an ice-cream cone. The term is a combination of *hokey-pokey*, an informal English word for ice-cream, plus *hat*, referring to the shape of the cone.

policies The **policies** of a large house, such as a mansion, are the enclosed grounds and gardens surrounding it. They are so called because they are the result of a deliberate *policy* of improvements to the building's surroundings.

polis (pronounced *po-liss*) The **polis** are the police: *If you phone the polis, we'll kill you.* A **polis** is a member of the police: *There was only one polis on duty.* The plural is also **polis**: *a hundred polis dressed in riot gear.*

pooch (rhymes with *butch*) A **pooch** is a pocket. The word is a Scots form of *pouch*.

pook A **pook** is a tuft of hair, wool, etc. sticking out from something. In some parts of West Central

Scotland a **pook** is a raised crease on a piece of material or item of clothing. Something which has a lot of these tufts or creases can be described as **pookie** or **pookit**. Earlier senses of the word mean to pluck, but its ultimate origin is unclear.

pope's eye or **popeseye** Pope's eye, or **pope's eye steak**, is a cut of rump steak for grilling or frying.

port-a-beul (pronounced *porsh-ta bee-al*) Another name for **mouth music**, the singing of simple or meaningless words to a tune originally intended as purely instrumental music. The name is originally Gaelic and means music from mouth.

postie A **postie** is a postman or postwoman.

potato scone or **tattie scone** A **potato scone** is a type of pancake made from a dough of mashed potato, fat and flour, which is rolled out thin and cooked on a griddle. They are usually cooked in a circular shape and then quartered. **Potato scones** are generally eaten on their own with butter or fried as an accompaniment to bacon, sausages, etc.

pot still A **pot still** is a type of still used in distilling malt whisky, in which heat is applied directly to the large metal pot which contains the **wash** (a liquid rather like weak beer). The vapour containing the alcohol passes out through the neck of the still and condenses back into liquid. The shape of the still and its neck is believed to influence the final taste of the whisky. Compare **patent still**.

pottit heid or **potted heid** Pottit heid is a traditional dish consisting of meat from the head of a cow or pig which has been boiled, chopped into small pieces, and covered in a jelly made from the stock. It is served cold.

pottit hough or **potted hough** (pronounced *hawCH*) Potted hough is a traditional dish very similar to **potted heid** but made with meat from the shin (**hough**) of a cow or pig.

poultice A **poultice** is a West and Central Scotland term for an obnoxious or disagreeable person: *She's a right wee poultice!*

pow (rhymes with *cow*) The **pow** is the head or skull: *a balding pow.*

precentor (pronounced *pree-sen-tor*) A **precentor** is an official in a Presbyterian church who leads the singing by singing each line of a psalm or hymn for the congregation to repeat. They are now found only in some of the smaller Presbyterian denominations which do not approve of the use of musical instruments in church. The word comes from Late Latin *praecentor*, from *prae* before plus *canere* to sing.

precognition (pronounced *prek-og-nish-un*) In Scots Law, a **precognition** is a preliminary statement made by a possible witness in a trial. It can be taken either by the procurator fiscal in order to ascertain if there is enough evidence to proceed with the case, or by a prosecuting or defending lawyer in order to prepare an adequate case. The term comes from the Late Latin *praecognitiō*, from *prae* before plus *cognoscere* to know or ascertain.

preen A **preen** is a pin.

prelim (pronounced *pree-lim*) A **prelim** is a school exam taken, usually in December or January, as practice for a public exam such as a Standard Grade or Higher which the candidate intends to sit later that year: *He failed his Maths prelim.* The term is a shortening of *preliminary examination*.

Presbyterian A **Presbyterian** Church, such as the Church of Scotland, is a Protestant Church which is governed not by bishops, but by a committee of **elders** at the level of individual churches, and by committees representing each church or area at a higher level. The doctrine of Presbyterian Churches is based on a modified form of Calvinism.

presbytery A **presbytery** is a council of a Presbyterian Church consisting of the minister and one elder from each congregation in an area which governs church affairs in that area: *He was found guilty of the charge by Ayr Presbytery and suspended from the Ministry indefinitely.* The word comes from the Greek *presbyterion*, which is from *presbuteros* an older man.

price In the Northeast, to say that something is **the price o** someone is to indicate that it serves them right and is exactly what they deserve.

prig To **prig** is a chiefly Northern word meaning to beg, plead, or beseech: *It had taken a lot of prigging to get her to go.*

Primus In the Episcopal Church, the **Primus** is a bishop chosen by his fellow bishops to preside over their meetings. While on some occasions he may act as spokesman for the Church, he does not have any greater spiritual authority than any other bishop. The title comes from the Latin *primus* meaning first.

principal or **principal teacher** In a Scottish school, a **principal** is a head of department: *the Principal Teacher of Mathematics.*

procurator fiscal The **procurator fiscal** in an area is a legal official who ascertains whether there is enough evidence in criminal cases for a trial to be held, acts as public prosecutor, and conducts investigations into sudden or suspicious deaths. **Procurator fiscals** are appointed by the **Lord Advocate**: *Two youths have been reported to the procurator fiscal in connection with an alleged car theft; She is the senior depute procurator fiscal in Glasgow.* It is often shortened to **fiscal**: *Fiscal Neil Macfadyen said there had been a row between the accused and one of the McKinlays.*

Proddie, Proddy or **Prod** A **Proddie** or **Prod** is a Central Scottish word for someone brought up as a member of one of the Protestant Churches. It is a term which is either derogatory or jocular depending on speaker and tone: *I'm a Catholic but most of my friends are Proddies.* Something which is **Proddie** is typical of Protestantism or associated with Protestants: *It has the reputation of being one of the most Proddie towns in Scotland.*

proof In Scots Law, **proof** has the additional meaning of a trial before a judge alone, without a jury: *The civil action proof began at Inverness Sheriff Court yesterday.*

provost (pronounced *prov-ost*) A **provost** is a councillor who acts as chairperson and civic head of certain district councils, equivalent to the mayor in some other countries. Until the early 1970s, the title was in general use as the title of the civic head of any burgh council, but it is now only used by a few district councils, with others using the title **convenor**. In the four main cities, the title **Lord Provost** is used: *Provost Margaret Miller of Dunfermline District Council.*

public school A **public school** in Scotland is one which was originally built and run by a local education authority, many of which are now primary schools. The term is no longer in current use, but the title can still be seen engraved on the front of many old school buildings: *Tullibody Public School.*

puckle A variant of **pickle**.

puddock A **puddock** is a frog or toad. The word comes from the Old English *pad* a toad, plus the diminutive ending *-ock*.

puggled To be **puggled** is to have reached a state where you feel that you can do nothing more, usually because of tiredness.

puggy or **puggie** ① In much of Scotland, a fruit machine or one-armed bandit is known as a **puggy**. **Puggy** is also sometimes used to mean a cash dispenser machine outside a bank or building society. Both of these senses are derived from an earlier, but still current, sense meaning the pool or kitty at a card game. ② Someone who is **fou as a puggie** is very drunk. ③ A **puggie** is an old name for a monkey. ④ To **get one's puggie up** or **take a puggie** is to lose one's temper.

puir (pronounced *pair*) or **pair** Puir means poor: *Of the puir beastie's tragic demise I shall say nothing.*

pulley A **pulley** is a type of clothes horse consisting of long parallel horizontal bars, that is attached to a rope and a system of pulleys, and can be hoisted up to just below the ceiling of a room (usually the kitchen). They are less common than they used to be, because of the advent of tumble driers, but can still be found in many older houses and flats. The rope used to support and raise or lower this is known as a **pulley rope**: *I spent the afternoon traipsing round Edinburgh trying to find a shop that sold pulley ropes.*

pump To **pump** is to break wind.

pun A **pun** is a pound (weight, not money): *a pun o mince.* The plural is also **pun**: *two pun o carrots.*

pure A noticeable feature of the speech of the Glasgow area is the extensive use of **pure** before an adjective as an intensifier meaning to the most extreme degree possible: *pure dead brilliant!*; *That's just pure ignorant, so it is.*

pursuer In Scots Law, a **pursuer** is the person who is bringing a civil court action. The equivalent in English law is the plaintiff: *You will receive a Service Document from the pursuer's solicitor, saying how much money you owe.*

purvey (rhymes with *curvy*) The food and drink provided after a funeral, at a wedding reception, etc. is known as the **purvey**. The word comes from the Old French *porveeir*, which in turn comes from the Latin *prōvidēre* to provide.

quaich (pronounced *kwayCH*) A **quaich** is a small shallow drinking cup, usually with two handles. They are now most commonly used as ornaments or trophies: *The final of the Ladies Quaich was postponed due to waterlogged conditions.* The word comes from the Gaelic *cuach* cup.

quair (rhymes with *swear*) A **quair** is a book. The word is most often found in the titles of literary works such as *The Kingis Quair* (c. 1424) by James the First, or *A Scots Quair* (1932-34) by Lewis Grassic Gibbon.

queenie A **queenie** is a type of shellfish (a queen scallop) fished for from harbours in the Southwest: *a stew of squid, queenies, monkfish and crab.*

queer Queer is often used to mean great or considerable: *There's a queer difference between what he's paid and what I get.*

queerie Any odd or strange person or thing may be called a **queerie**: *She's a bit of a queerie, that yin.*

queet A **queet** is a Northeastern name for an ankle. The word is a local form of the older Scots *cuit*, which comes from the Middle Dutch *cote* an ankle.

quine (rhymes with *twine*) or **quean** (pronounced

queen) In the Northeast a **quine** is a young unmarried woman or girl. **Quean** is a chiefly literary variant: *He had mairrit on a quine fae Torry.* The word comes from the Old English *cwene* a woman.

quite A **quite** is a Northeastern word for a petticoat or underskirt. It is a local form of *coat*.

quoted In the Glasgow area **quoted** means respected or admired: *the highly quoted young lion from the BBC.*

ra Ra is a broad Glaswegian word meaning the: *Gaun tae ra gemme ra morra?*

Rab Ha (pronounced *haw*) In parts of the West of Scotland, someone who is greedy or has a large appetite may be described as a **Rab Ha**: *He's a right Rab Ha*. The term alludes to *Robert Hall*, a legendary glutton, who died in Glasgow in 1843.

radge, raj, radgie or **rajie** To be or go **radge** is to act in a wild or crazy manner, either because that is an intrinsic character trait, or because carried away by a strong emotion such as anger or lust: *He went totally radge when he heard what I'd done; Stop that, ya rajie wee bastard!* A **radge** is someone who behaves in a wild or irrational way: *D'ye ken whit the radge did next?* The word, which is used in Eastern Scotland, particularly in the Edinburgh area, is probably a variant of **rage**, although it may be influenced by the Romany **raj** stupid or crazy.

raggle A **raggle** or **ragglin** is a groove cut in a piece of stone or wood to enable another piece to fit into it, especially one to hold the edge of a roof. To **raggle** a piece of stone or wood is to cut such a groove in it. The word is probably ultimately from the Latin **rēgula**, meaning a straight piece of wood, but its exact derivation is unclear.

ragnail A **ragnail** is a narrow spike of loose skin or broken nail beside a finger nail.

raivel (rhymes with *navel*) To **raivel** is to become tangled or confused. Something which is **raivelt** is tangled or confused. To be **raivelt** is to be baffled or confused: *His mind's aa raivelt.* The word is a Scots form of *ravel* to tangle (which is now most commonly encountered as a component of *unravel*).

raj, rajie See **radge**.

ramgunshoch (pronounced *ram-gun-shoCH*) A **ramgunshoch** person is unpleasantly rough, coarse and bad-tempered in manner; a splendid sounding, if rare, word.

rammy A **rammy** is a noisy fight or brawl involving a number of people: *Tempers flared, leading to a rammy involving groups of youths from the two towns.* The word possibly comes from the earlier Scots *rammle* a row or uproar.

ramstam (pronounced *ram-stam*) To do something **ramstam** is to do it in a hurried and clumsy way, launching headlong into it without proper care or thought: *She went at it ramstam.*

randan (pronounced *ran-dan*) To be **on the randan** is to be on a spree and having a wild or dissolute good time, frequently but not necessarily one involving a lot of alcohol: *They were out on the randan to celebrate the end of term.* **Randan** is probably a variant of *random*.

rant A **rant** is a lively traditional tune, particularly one suitable for use as dance music: *McPherson's Rant.*

rasp A **rasp** is a raspberry.

rax To **rax** is to stretch one's body or a part of one's body: *He raxed out his arm.* To **rax** something is to fetch it or give it to someone else with an outstretched arm: *Rax us ower the salt.* To **rax** a limb can also be to sprain or wrench it by stretching or turning it too far or too energetically. The word comes from the Old English *raxan* to stretch.

reamin Something which is **reamin** or **reamin fou** is full to the point of overflowing.

rector In some of the Scottish Universities, the **rector** is a person elected by the students to act as honorary head of the University, usually for a period of three years: *A move was made to stop the elected Rector of Edinburgh University from chairing meetings of the University Court.* In some secondary schools, the headteacher is also known as the **rector**: *the Rector of Harris Academy; the deputy rector.*

red biddy **Red biddy** is a mixture of cheap red wine and methylated spirits: *an old jakie clasping his bottle of red biddy.*

redd To **redd** or **redd up** a place is to clear or tidy it up: *I must get round to redding up that cupboard sometime.* The past of **redd** can be either **redded** or **redd**. To give a place a **redd** or **redd up** is to tidy it up: *We'll need to give the front room a good redd up before your mother comes.* The term probably comes from Middle Dutch or Low German.

reek To **reek** is to give off smoke: *reeking lums*. **Reek** is smoke: *peat reek*. The word is related to the German *Rauch* smoke and *rauchen* to smoke.

reekin Someone who is **reekin** is very angry: *I was pure reekin when I heard I'd failed.*

reel A **reel** is a type of fast dance for groups of dancers, each made up of a number of couples, or a piece of music in quadruple time for such a dance: *an eightsome reel.*

reese (rhymes with *please*) To **reese** is a chiefly Northern word meaning to praise or extol: *He aye reesed the wifie's bannocks.*

reestit Food that has been **reestit** has been cured by drying, or smoking it. **Reestit mutton** is a Shetland speciality, a type of wind-dried mutton which is used for making soup and has good keeping qualities. The word is probably of Scandanavian origin: compare the Norwegian and Danish *riste* to broil or grill.

refreshment A **refreshment** is a euphemism for an alcoholic drink: *His fondness for a wee refreshment was known throughout the company.* To say that someone is **refreshed** is a euphemistic way of saying that they are drunk.

Region A **Region** was one of the nine larger units of local government which mainland Scotland was divided into between 1975 and 1996, and which was responsible for education, social work, and roads and transport. Each Region was subdivided into a number of Districts, each of which was controlled by a separate council.

Both Regions and Districts have since been replaced by single-tier local councils of which there are twenty nine: *Tayside Region*. Compare **District** and **Islands Council**.

Regional Something which is **Regional** is connected with a local government Region: *Lothian Regional Council*; *the forthcoming Regional elections*.

Renfrewshire (pronounced *ren-froo-sher* or *ren-froo-shire*) **Renfrewhire** is an area, and former county, of West Central Scotland, on the south bank of the Clyde west of Glasgow. It is now administered by three single-tier local councils: Renfrewshire, East Renfrewshire, and Inverclyde.

Reporter The **Reporter to the Children's Panel** is the official responsible for arranging and conducting cases to be considered by a Children's Hearing. See **Children's Hearing**.

rerr Rerr is a broad Glaswegian form of rare (in the sense: great or excellent): *that wis rerr; a rerr terr*.

reset (when a noun, pronounced *ree-set*) **Reset** is the crime of receiving or selling stolen goods: *He faced charges involving reset, break-ins and theft; She admitted the reset of a stolen video recorder*. (when a verb, pronounced *ree-set*) To **reset** something which has been stolen is to receive or sell it: *He pled guilty to resetting three cars which had been stolen last September*. The past is also **reset**. The word comes from the Old French *receter*, which ultimately comes from the Latin *recipere* to receive.

retiral A **retiral** is the act of retiring from a job or position: *He announced his retiral from the post of vice-convener*.

rhinn (pronounced *rin*) A **rhinn** is a headland or promontory. Nowadays the word is only seen in place names such as *the Rhinns of Galloway* (often known simply as *the Rhinns*) or *the Rhinns of Islay*. The word comes from Gaelic *rinn*.

rhone, rhonepipe (pronounced *roan*) See **rone** and **ronepipe**.

richt (pronounced *riCHt*) **Richt** means right: *What richt hae the Tories tae rin Scotlan on the votes o the English?*; *a richt gubbing.*

rickle A **rickle** is a loose heap or pile of things: *a rickle of stones.* Someone who is unhealthily thin may be described as **a rickle of banes**. The word is probably Scandinavian in origin.

riddy A **riddy** is a blush of embarrassment, or a situation which causes great embarrassment: *I didn't recognize her with that new hairdo. Whit a riddy!* The word is from *rid*, a Scottish pronunciation of **red**.

Riding The **Common Riding** or **Riding of the Marches** is an annual festival held in several towns in Southeast Scotland, in which townspeople ceremonially ride round the town boundaries. The day on which this takes place is often an important local holiday. Some places, for instance, Hawick, Selkirk and Langholm, know the ceremony as the **Common Riding**, while others such as Peebles, Annan and Lanark use the name **Riding of the Marches**.

rift To **rift** is to belch. A **rift** is a belch.

rig A **rig** is a long strip of cultivated or ploughed land: *corn rigs.* The word, which because of changes in farming methods is not now common, is a variant of *ridge.* See also **runrig**.

right The phrase **that will be right** or **that'll be right** is often used contemptuously to dismiss the preceding statement as untrue or ludicrously improbable: *An accident, he says. That'll be right!* See also **shining bright**.

rive To **rive** something is to pull or tug it firmly, or to tear it by pulling at it. A **rive** is a firm pull or tug.

roasted cheese Roasted cheese is the usual Scottish name for the dish consisting of bread which is toasted on one side, then has cheese put on the other side which is then toasted in turn. Elsewhere it is generally known as toasted cheese.

roch (pronounced *roCH*) **Roch** means rough: *Yon's a gey roch pub.*

rodden A **rodden** is a Northern name for a rowan berry or, less often, for a rowan tree. Compare **rowan**. The name is probably Scandanavian in origin and related to the English word *red.*

rone or **rhone** A **rone** is one of the gutters along the edge of a roof, for carrying away rainwater. It is also short for **ronepipe**. The origin of the word is not clear, but it may be connected with *run.*

ronepipe or **rhonepipe** A **ronepipe** is one of the drain pipes running from the gutter on a roof to the ground.

roon Roon means round.

roost ① Roost is rust. Something which is **roosty** is rusty. ② A **roost** is a powerful current caused by conflicting tides, found around Orkney and Shetland: *the battering seas that fill Sumburgh Roost during ferocious winter gales.* This sense of the word is from the Old Norse *röst*.

Ross and Cromarty Ross and Cromarty is the area of Northern Scotland which forms the southern part of the large peninsula stretching north from the western end of the Moray Firth near Inverness. The former county of the same name also included the northern part of the island of Lewis and Harris in the Outer Hebrides.

roup (pronounced *rowp*) A **roup** is an auction. To sell things **by roup** is to auction them: *The said goods and effects will be sold by public roup.* These senses have developed from an earlier meaning of **roup**, to shout or call, which comes from the Old Norse *raupa* to brag or boast.

rouser (pronounced *rooz-er*) A **rouser** is a chiefly Northeastern term for a watering-can. The word comes via the Middle English *arrouse* from Old French *arrouser* to sprinkle or bedew.

rowan (first syllable rhymes with *now*) A **rowan** is a type of slender tree which has small white flowers in spring and bright red berries in early Autumn; it is known elsewhere as the mountain ash: *the beautiful autumn colours of the rowans and silver birches.* The fruit of this tree is known either as a **rowan** or as a **rowan berry**. Compare **rodden**. The word is of Scandinavian origin.

rowie (first syllable rhymes with *now*) **Rowie** and **buttery rowie** are Northeastern names for the type of flaky, butter-rich, bread roll, originally from Aberdeen, which is generally called a **buttery** elsewhere in Scotland.

Roxburgh **Roxburgh** or **Roxburghshire** is a former inland county of Southeastern Scotland, on the border with England. It is now administered by Borders single-tier local council.

Royal and Ancient The **Royal and Ancient** is a golf club in St Andrews in Fife which functions as the sport's ruling body: *He said that he thought all the courses which the Royal and Ancient selected for the Open were great.*

royal burgh A **royal burgh** is a **burgh** (a town formerly governed by its own council) which was given its charter by the monarch: *New Galloway, the smallest Royal Burgh in Scotland.*

Royal Deeside **Royal Deeside** is the popular name for the area of Aberdeenshire on the banks of the River Dee around Ballater and Braemar where the British royal family has had a holiday home at Balmoral since 1848.

rubber-ear To **rubber-ear** someone is a Glasgow term meaning to ignore or snub a person by pretending not to have heard them: *I said hello to him but he just rubber-eared me.* To **give someone the rubber ear** is to ignore them in this way.

rumgumption (pronounced *rum-gum-shun*) or **rummle-gumption** Rumgumption is common sense: *He hadn't even the rumgumption to say where he was going.*

rummle (rhymes with *pummel*) **Rummle** means rumble: *a rummle o thunder.* To **rummle** is to go, move, or search through something in a vigorous but clumsy way: *She rummled through the drawer looking for the scissors.* A **rummle** is a vigorous but clumsy movement or search, or a person who is doing something in such a way: *Don't be such a rummle!* In sports such as football, to **rummle up** opposing players is to try to put them off by hard physical play: *Just get in there and rummle up that big centre-half.*

rummlethump (pronounced *rum-l-thump*) or **rummledethump** (pronounced *rum-l-dee-thump*) **Rummlethump** is a dish made of cabbage mixed into mashed potatoes.

runkle To **runkle** something is to crease or crumple it: *His jacket was all runkled when he took it down from the locker.*

runrig (pronounced *run-rig*) **Runrig** was a former landholding system in which tenants were allocated a number of strips of land (**rigs**) by lot for a year, so that, over a long period of time, everyone would have an equal share of fertile and poor land. The system fell into disuse in the late 18th century: *Next to the abandoned township, the ground was still ridged with old runrig strips.*

sae (pronounced *say*) **Sae** means so: *It's no sae bad.*

saft Anything or anyone **saft** is soft: *He's too saft in the heid tae ken whit we're on aboot.*

saftie ① In some areas, chiefly in the Northeast, slippers are known as **safties**. ② A **saftie** is also a Northeastern name for a soft bread roll, a bap, as distinct from a **rowie**.

sair A part of the body which is **sair** is aching and painful: *a sair heid.* Something which is **a sair fecht** involves a great deal of effort or is a struggle.

sair heidie A **sair heidie** is a type of small plain sponge cake with a paper wrapper round the lower part of it, found in the Northeast. The name alludes to the similarity between the paper wrapper and a bandage.

sair on or **sore on** To be **sair on** something is to use it in such a way that it is quickly worn out or used up: *She's awful sair on her clothes; This would be a good car if it wasn't so sore on the petrol.*

sang A **sang** is a song. **The end of an auld sang** is the end of any long-established tradition or institution. The phrase alludes to the Earl of Seafield's description of the Act of Union in 1707 which led to the end of an independent Scottish Parliament as *an end of an auld song*.

sannies In much of Central Scotland, gym-shoes or plimsolls are frequently referred to as **sannies**. The word is a shortening of *sandshoes*.

sapple To **sapple** something is to rinse or wash it out. **Sapple** or **sapples** is a word for a soapy lather. Both senses of the word are most commonly used in Central Scotland.

sapsy Someone who is **sapsy** is soft and unable to stand up for themselves or is excessively sentimental. A **sapsy** is someone who is sapsy. Both senses of this mainly West Central Scottish word are frequently used of small children. The word comes from *saps*, a Scottish form of the English sops meaning food soaked in a liquid before eating to soften it, and is equivalent to the English *soppy*.

sark A **sark** is a slightly old-fashioned word for a man's shirt. **Sark** formerly also meant a woman's chemise or slip, as in Burn's poem "Tam O' Shanter" where the young and attractive witch is described as wearing only a "cutty sark", a short shift.

sarking The planks, boards, or felt cladding placed over the rafters of a roof under the tiles or slates is known in Scotland as the **sarking**. The term ultimately comes from *sark*, via an earlier meaning of material for making shirts.

Sassenach (pronounced *sass-en-aCH*) A **Sassenach** is an informal, often jocular, name for an English person, frequently thought of as being a typical Scots word but in fact very rarely used seriously: *a bit of fun at this gullible Sassenach's expense.* Strictly speaking, the Lowland Scots are **Sassenachs** as well, since the word originally meant anyone who wasn't a Gaelic-speaking Highlander. It comes from the Gaelic *Sassunach* a Saxon.

sax In some parts of Northern Scotland, the word **sax** is used instead of six.

scaffie or **scaffy** A **scaffie** is a street-sweeper or dustman. The word is a shortened form of *scavenger.*

scart To **scart** is to scratch or scrape. A **scart** is a scratch or scrape.

scaur (rhymes with *war*) or **scar** A **scaur** is an area of steep exposed rock on a hillside. **Scaur** is sometimes used in the name of hills which have steep rocky faces, such as *Scaur Hill* or *Blackhope Scar.*

SCE SCE is short for Scottish Certificate of Education, the main Scottish national secondary-school qualifications, which serve both as school-leaving qualifications and as qualifying exams for university and college. An **SCE** exam is taken in an individual subject, either at **Standard Grade** or as a **Higher**.

schedule A **schedule** is a document stating the price, size and number of rooms, and other details of a house or flat for sale which the estate agent or solicitor handling the sale gives to prospective buyers.

scheme A **scheme**, sometimes referred to more formally as a **housing scheme**, is a housing estate, particularly one built by a local council or other public sector organization: *a sprawling housing scheme just north of the town centre*; *The councillor, who lives in the scheme herself, claimed residents were angry that convicted housebreakers were treated so leniently.*

schemie A **schemie** is an informal name for someone who lives on one of the large council housing estates which are found on the outskirts of many Scottish towns. In some areas the term is considered rather derogatory.

sclaff To **sclaff** something is to hit it a glancing blow with something flat. In golf to **sclaff** a shot is to mishit the ball because the head of the club has hit the ground a glancing blow before hitting the ball. A **sclaff** is a slap or glancing blow, or a mishit shot at golf where the club hits the ground before the ball. The word is onomatopoeic in origin.

scliff See **skliff**.

scone (rhymes with *gone*) If a person looks as if someone has **stolen their scone**, they look miserable or depressed: *Who's stolen your scone, then?*

scooby In Glasgow, to **not have a scooby** about something is to know nothing at all about it: *She's not got a scooby what we're talking about, has she?* **Scooby** is short for *Scooby Doo*, rhyming slang for clue (in the sense "the slightest idea"), *Scooby Doo* being a cartoon dog who appeared in a popular children's television series first broadcast in the U.K. in the late 1960s.

scoor To **scoor** something is to clean it by vigourous scrubbing: *to scoor oot a pan.* To **scoor** also means to roughen by scrubbing or scraping.

scoosh or **skoosh** To **scoosh** is to squirt or spurt: *He scooshed me with a water pistol; Water came scooshing out of the tap.* A **scoosh** is a squirt or spurt of liquid. **Scoosh** is also any fizzy soft drink, such as lemonade. Someone who finds a particular task or problem very easy to deal with might describe it informally as **a scoosh** or a **scoosh case**: *Buying a new house in the current market is easy, a scoosh case.* To **scoosh it** is to do or win something easily, without having to make a serious effort: *At home to Stenhousemuir in the next round? Ach, we'll scoosh it.*

scoosher or **skoosher** A **scoosher** is any of various devices for squirting or spraying water, such as one of the windscreen washers on a car.

Scot A **Scot** is a person from Scotland: this term is preferred in Scotland to "Scotsman" or "Scotswoman". Historically, the **Scots** were a tribe of Celtic raiders from Ireland who settled in what is now Argyll during the 5th and 6th centuries.

Scotch **Scotch** is another word for **Scottish** or **Scots**. It is not used (and in fact actively disliked) in Scotland itself, except in certain fixed expressions, most of which have to do with food: *Scotch broth; prime Scotch beef.* **Scotch** or **Scotch whisky** is whisky made in Scotland. See **whisky**.

Scotland The name **Scotland** generally refers to one of the countries which form the United Kingdom. Geographically, it consists of the northern section of the island of Great Britain, plus many offshore islands. The south of Scotland (**the Southern Uplands**) is hilly, north of that lies a central Lowland area where most of the population live, and the northern half of the country consists largely of low mountains (**the Highlands**). The Gulf Stream, an ocean current which carries warm water up from the Caribbean past the Scottish coast, ensures that Scotland is warmer than many other countries on the same latitude (Edinburgh is as far north as Moscow, and Wick as far north as Juneau, the capital of Alaska). The proximity of the Atlantic Ocean and the prevalence of westerly winds results in a fairly high rainfall all year round. Scotland was an independent kingdom until 1603, when the thrones of Scotland and England were united by James the VI of Scotland succeeding to the English throne following the death of Queen Elizabeth of England. The Scottish and English parliaments agreed to merge in 1707. Since then Scotland has been in the slightly strange constitutional position of having its own independent legal, educational, and religious systems, but having the laws governing these made by a British parliament in which Scottish MPs are but a small minority. In recent years this has caused some ill-feeling because in the last few elections Scottish voters have overwhelmingly voted for MPs belonging to parties other than the one in power in Britain. Over the years many people have wanted Scotland either to have more control over its internal affairs or to leave the United Kingdom altogether. In Orkney and Shetland, however, the term **Scotland** is often used to mean the rest of Scotland, excluding the Orkney and Shetland Isles.

Scots Something or someone which is **Scots** comes from Scotland. In current Scots use, both **Scots** or **Scottish** are regarded as acceptable usage. **Scots** is the language spoken, in a variety of forms, by the majority of people who live in Scotland. It is descended from the Germanic dialect spoken by the Anglo-Saxon people who settled in Southeast Scotland in the 7th century. More information about the history and dialects of **Scots** can be found in the Introduction to this dictionary. See also **Doric** and **Lallans**.

Scots Law Scotland has a different legal system from the rest of the United Kingdom, based on the principles of **Scots Law**. In common with much of the rest of Europe, the law in Scotland is based on principles of Roman or civil law (ie based on the interpretation of fundamental principles), rather than the common law (based on what has been decided in similar cases in the past) which forms the basis of the legal systems of England and the USA. To the non-expert, the main differences between Scots and English Law are the different names given to various courts and officials, the presence of 15 people on a Scottish jury, and the existence in Scotland of the verdict of **not proven**.

Scotticism A **Scotticism** is a distinctively Scottish word or expression used in speaking English. It generally refers to words and phrases which Scots think of as standard English without realising that they are just Scottish, such as "the messages" or "split-new", rather than to more overtly Scottish terms.

Scottish A **Scottish** person or thing comes from Scotland. In Orkney and Shetland, **Scottish** often means from the Scottish mainland rather than from one of the Orkney or Shetland Isles.

Scottish Office The **Scottish Office** is the section of the British Government and Civil Service which deals with Scottish affairs.

SCOTVEC A **SCOTVEC** course or qualification is one offered or awarded by the **Scottish Vocational and Educational Council**. SCOTVEC courses cover a wide range of subjects including science, engineering, computing, foreign languages, typing and other office skills, music, building, and the tourism industry. Courses are made up of a number of self-contained "modules" and are generally studied in the later years of secondary school or at a further education college. They tend to be less academic and more vocational than **Highers**: *The College offers a programme of SCOTVEC modules in Dental Technology.*

scratcher A **scratcher** is a slang term for a bed: *I'm rarely out of my scratcher before ten on a Saturday.*

scrieve or **screive** (pronounced *skreev*) To **scrieve** is to write. **Scrieve** is now literary or slightly old-fashioned, and sometimes has the implication of writing fluently or at length without really having much to say. It probably ultimately comes from the Latin word *scribere* to write, which is also the root of the English *scribe*.

scud ① A **scud** is a slap or smack, and hence to **scud** someone is to slap or smack them: *Are you wanting a scud on the lug?* ② If someone is **in the scud** or, even more shockingly, **in the bare scud**, they are naked: *She was wandering around the house in the bare scud.*

scuddie or **scuddy** To be **scuddie** is to be naked.

scunner If something **scunners** you it irritates or disgusts you greatly. To be **scunnered** by someone or something is to be sickened or disgusted by it, either because it is unpleasant or because you are utterly fed up with it: *I'm scunnered with having to get up at six every morning.* A **scunner** can be either the feeling of disgust or loathing brought about by someone or something unpleasant (usually in the phrase *to take a scunner to*), or the person, object or situation which causes this feeling: *I took a scunner to Shakespeare when I had to study him at Uni; This weather's a right scunner, isn't it?*

scutter Scutter is a Northern word with a number of related meanings. To **scutter** is to do something in a messy and slapdash way. To **scutter** or **scutter about** is to waste time or dawdle. A **scutter** is an awkward but boring or trivial piece of work. It is possibly a variant of *skitter*.

scutterie A **scutterie** job or task is one which is awkward, fiddly and time-consuming: a Northeastern word.

SED The **SED** is the **Scottish Education Department**.

sederunt (pronounced *sid-dare-unt*) The **sederunt** is the formal name for the list of people present at a meeting. It comes from the Latin *sēdērunt* they were sitting, and ultimately from *sedēre*, the Latin word meaning to sit.

see ① In the Glasgow area, **see** is commonly used to introduce a subject of conversation: *See thae balloons in head office?* It is possible, and indeed fairly common, to string together a number of phrases beginning with **see** to form a statement: *See ma sister? See her man? See bevvied?* **See** is also used in a number of common Scottish idioms. **See if** means supposing that or if it is the case that: *See if we're to be there by seven, when do we have to leave here?*; *See if that wean disnae shut up, Ah'll belt him one.* If you have **seen yourself** doing something, you are aware of having done it in the past: *I've seen me having to wait half-an-hour for a bus.* ② To **see** someone something is to give them it: *See's ower the paper.*

sel One's **sel** is one's self: frequently used in combination, as in *masel* or *hersel*: *Let him do it himsel; She's no been just hersel since the accident.*

selkie or **silkie** A **selkie** is a name, now mainly used in Northern Scotland for a seal. In folklore, a **selkie** is a mythical creature which takes on the form of a seal in the sea and a human on land.

Selkirk bannock (pronounced *sell-kirk ban-nok*) See **bannock**.

Selkirkshire (pronounced *sell-kirk-sher* or *sell-kirk-shire*) **Selkirkshire** is a former inland county of Southeastern Scotland. It is now administered by Borders single-tier local council.

selt Selt is a Scottish past form of sell, often used instead of sold.

semmit (pronounced *sim-mit* or *sem-mit*) or **simmit** A **semmit** is a vest: *No wonder you're cold. Away and put your semmit on.*

sept A sept is one of the branches into which some clans are divided. The word is possibly a variant of *sect*.

session Short for **kirk session**.

session clerk A **session clerk** is the secretary of a **kirk session**.

set blow In shinty, a **set blow** is a penalty stroke awarded to a team when the opposing team have committed a foul. The player taking the set blow cannot hit the ball again until another player has touched it, and cannot score directly from the set blow.

sett A sett is the pattern of coloured squares and lines which is repeated throughout a tartan.

SFA The SFA is the **Scottish Football Association**.

sgian-dhu (pronounced *skee-an-doo*) Same as **skean-dhu**.

Sgionaich or **Sgitheanaich** (pronounced *skee-on-*

aCH) A **Sgionaich** is a person from Skye. The word was originally Gaelic and comes from **Sgiathanach**, the Gaelic name for Skye.

sharger (pronounced *sharg-er*) A **sharger** is a Northeastern term for a weak, puny, or stunted-looking person or animal. Someone or something which is **shargert** or **shargered** is weak, puny, or stunted looking. The word comes from the Gaelic *searg* a puny creature.

sharn or **shairn** Sharn is dung, especially the dung of cattle.

sharny or **shairny** Something which is **sharny** is covered in, or smeared with, dung.

shauchle (pronounced *shawCH-l*) To **shauchle** is to walk slowly and awkwardly without lifting one's feet properly: *Some old guy was shauchling along the street.*

shaw The **shaws** of a plant on which root vegetables such as potatoes or turnips grow are the leaves and stalks which are visible above ground. To **shaw** fruit or vegetables such as potatoes is to remove the stalks and leaves. The term comes from an earlier sense of *shaw*, to show.

shed A **shed** is a parting in someone's hair. The word comes from the Old English *sceadan* to separate.

sheen A Northeastern form of **shin** (shoes).

sheepy meh (rhymes with *yeah*) or **sheepy mae** A **sheepy meh** is a child's name for a sheep. In some parts of Scotland, the white flowers of clover are known as

sheepy mehs because their white, vaguely woolly, appearance is reminiscent of sheep seen from a distance.

sheltie A **Shetland pony** is often referred to informally as a **sheltie**. The word probably comes from the Orkney dialect *sjalti*, which in turn comes from Old Norse *Hjalti* a Shetlander, *Hjaltland* being the Viking name for Shetland.

shenachie (pronounced *shen-aCH-ee*) A **shenachie** is someone who has an extensive knowledge of Gaelic history and folktales, originally someone employed by a clan chief to record the history of the clan. The word comes from Gaelic, where it is spelt *seanachaidh*.

Sheriff A **Sheriff** is a legal officer whose chief duty is to sit as a judge in a **Sheriff Court**.

Sheriff Clerk A **Sheriff Clerk** is a person employed to look after the administrative work involved in the running of a **Sheriff Court**.

Sheriff Court A **Sheriff Court** is a court which deals with all but the most serious crimes and with most civil actions. The maximum sentence that can be imposed at a Sheriff Court is three years' imprisonment. There are **Sheriff Courts** in most of the main Scottish towns: *He was fined £450 at Banff Sheriff Court.*

sheriff officer A **sheriff officer** is someone who is employed to do tasks such as delivering summons and collecting debts on behalf of a Sheriff: *They were arrested for stopping sheriff officers seizing household goods for a warrant sale.*

Sheriff Principal A **Sheriff Principal** is the chief Sheriff of an area.

sherrackin (pronounced *sher-ack-in*) A variant spelling of **shirrackin**.

Shetland **Shetland**, also known as **the Shetland Isles** or **Islands**, is a group of around 100 islands, about 20 of which are inhabited, off the North coast of Scotland, north of Orkney.

Shetlander A **Shetlander** is a person from Shetland.

Shetland pony A **Shetland pony** is a type of very small sturdy pony with a long shaggy mane and tail, first bred on the Shetland Isles.

sheugh or **sheuch** (pronounced *shuCH*) A **sheugh** is a gutter or ditch for drainage: *a long sheugh which his father had dug with a pick and shovel*. The word comes from the Middle English *sogh* a swamp.

shieling (pronounced *sheel-ing*) A **shieling** is a rough, sometimes temporary, hut or shelter used by people looking after farm animals on high or remote ground, especially in days gone by: *Across the loch stood an abandoned shieling, its roof timbers gaping*. The word comes from the Middle English *shale* a hut.

shilling Scottish beers are sometimes classified according to the number of **shillings** of duty that was formerly payable on a barrel. The stronger the beer was, the higher the duty on it. This system of describing beers dropped out of use in the 1950s, but was reintroduced in the 1970s, purely as an indication of the general character of a beer and with no relation to the duty actually paid. Roughly speaking, **sixty shilling** is light beer, **seventy shilling** is heavy, and **eighty shilling** is export. In speech, the word shilling is frequently implied rather than stated: *Two pints of eighty and a lager, please.*

shilpit Someone who is **shilpit** is thin and weak-looking, as if they are underfed or in poor health.

shin, sheen or **shoon** Shin is a Scots plural of shoe: *Ma new shin are nippin.*

shining bright In the Glasgow area, the phrase **that will be shining bright**, often shortened to **that'll be shining** is used to indicate that the speaker thinks that what has just been said is either untrue or highly unlikely: *The Jags win the League? Aye, that'll be shining bright.* It is rhyming slang for *right* (in the sense "correct", "true").

shinty Shinty is a sport in which two teams of 12 players attempt to hit a ball into the opposing team's goal using a stick called a **caman**. Unlike in hockey, the players are allowed to hit the ball over head height, and can use both sides of the stick. Players are not allowed to kick, catch, or throw the ball, although the goalkeeper on each side is allowed to block shots with his hands. Attacking players cannot enter a 10 yard semicircle around their opponents' goal unless the ball is already in that area. Shinty is mainly played in the Highlands and by men. The word **shinty** is also occasionally used to refer to the stick used by the players. The name is possibly from the Gaelic *sinteag* to leap.

Shire ① East Stirling football club are nicknamed **Shire**. The club's full name is *East Stirlingshire*. (They play in Falkirk, which was formerly in Stirlingshire, not in Stirling town). ② In Galloway, **Wigtownshire** is often referred to simply as **the Shire**, in contrast to the neighbouring **Stewartry of Kirkcudbright**, which is known as **the Stewartry**.

shirrackin (pronounced *shir-ak-in*) or **sherrackin** A **shirrickin** is a severe scolding or telling-off, especially one conducted in public and intended to humiliate the recipient or serve as a warning to other people. The word is mainly heard in and around Glasgow: *The weans got a right shirrackin for no sayin where they were gaun.*

shite Shite means the same as shit.

shoogle To **shoogle** is to shake, sway, or rock from side to side, or to make something shake, sway, or rock from side to side: *The trailer shoogled alarmingly as we drove up the track; He shoogled his son awake.* A **shoogle** is a shake, push or nudge: *Give me a shoogle if I look like falling asleep.* The word comes from the earlier *shog* to shake or sway, and is apparently related to the German *schaukeln* to swing or rock.

shoogly Something which is **shoogly** is shaky, unsteady or wobbly: *a shoogly table*. To tell someone that their **jaicket is on a shoogly nail** or **peg** is to say that they are in danger of losing their job: *That's the second big* *order we've lost this month. The boss's jaicket must be on a shoogly peg.*

shoon A variant form of **shin**, the Scots plural of shoes.

shoother (pronounced *shooTH-er*) or **shooder** A **shoother** is a shoulder.

shortie Shortbread is often informally referred to as **shortie**.

shot A **shot** on or of something is temporary use of it, a go or turn on it: *Can I have a shot of your bike?*

shows The **shows** is a name given in Central and Southern Scotland to a funfair with roundabouts, dodgems, etc: *Grannie says she'll take me to the shows on Saturday.*

shy A **shy** is an informal name for a throw-in at football: *He kicked the ball out of the park, then tried to take the shy himself.*

sic (pronounced *sik*) **Sic** is an old-fashioned or literary word meaning such: *He gied me sic a fricht.*

siccar or **sicker** **Siccar** is an old-fashioned word meaning sure or certain: *I'll mak siccar.* The word comes via Middle English from the Latin *sēcūrus* meaning secure.

sicht (pronounced *siCHt*) A **sicht** is a sight: *an awfu sicht.*

sic-like **Sic-like** is an old-fashioned or literary word meaning such-like or similar things: *ribbons and bows and sic-like.*

sideyways or **sidieways** Sideyways means sideways: *The door's that wee you can only get through sideyways.*

silkie Another way of spelling **selkie**.

siller Siller is a slightly old-fashioned word for money or silver: *He'd paid guid siller for it*; *Britain's oldest surviving sporting trophy, the Siller Gun presented to the town by King James VI.*

simmer dim The **simmer dim** is the night-long twilight found in Orkney and Shetland in midsummer, when dusk runs more or less directly into dawn and it is never truly dark.

simmit Same as **semmit**.

single In a fish-and-chip shop, a **single** fish, pie, etc, is one served by itself without chips: *A fish supper and a single fish, please.*

single end A **single end** is a house or flat consisting of one room only, without even an inside toilet. They are no longer common.

skail If a building, such as a factory, pub, or hall **skails**, it empties at the end of a shift, closing time, etc, and the people in it head off in different directions: *The road's aye busy when the bingo's skailing.* When the people who have been in a building, at a meeting, and so forth, leave at the end of the day or the end of an event, they are also said to **skail**. To **skail** also means to spill: *Watch you don't skail my pint!*

skean-dhu or **sgian-dhu** (pronounced *skee*-an-doo) A

skean-dhu is a type of short-bladed knife or dagger with a black hilt, which is often worn at the outside top of the right sock as part of a man's Highland dress. The word is from the Gaelic *sgian-dubh* meaning black knife.

skeich (pronounced *skeeCH*) A **skeich** person or animal is in an excited, lively but easily upset mood: a word often used of young children. **Skeich** is also used to describe an elderly but fit and active person. The word is related to the Old English *scéoh* shy.

skelf A **skelf** is the name given in some areas, mainly Central Scotland and the Far North, to a splinter of wood, especially one which has become embedded in someone's skin. Other names for this include **spelk** and **stob**. A **skelf** is also a small thin person: *What does a wee skelf of a lassie like her need to diet for?*

skellie or **skelly** If someone is **skellie** or **skellie-eyed**, they have a squint in their eye: *Ye'll go skellie if ye sit and play thae video games aw day.* Something which is **skellie** is askew or out of its proper alignment. Both senses of the word are used mainly in Central and Southern Scotland.

skelp A **skelp** is a smack or slap: *All that boy needs is a good skelp.* To **skelp** someone is to smack or slap them. To **skelp** is also to move or go quickly: *He went skelping down the road after the bus.*

skerry A **skerry** is a rock or small rocky island in the sea, often one which is covered by water at high tide. Most **skerries** are in Orkney or Shetland, and the word is often used in the name of rocky islands such as the *Pentland Skerries.*

skiddle To **skiddle** is to splash or spill water or another liquid or to play about splashily with water, as children are fond of doing. In the Glasgow area **skiddle about** can also mean to mess around or busy oneself with trivial tasks. A **skiddle** is a wet splashed or spilled mess, or a period of time spent playing about with water. It comes from *scuddler*, an old word for a kitchen-boy, which is thought to come via Old French from *scutella*, the Latin word for a dish or pan.

skinnymalink (pronounced *skin-ee-ma-link*) or **skinnymalinkie** (pronounced *skin-ee-ma-link-ee*) A **skinnymalink** is an informal, slightly jocular, name for any very thin person or animal, as in the children's rhyme which begins *skinnymalinkie long-legs, big banana feet*.

skint Someone who has **skint** their knee or another part of their body, or has a **skint** knee etc, has grazed or skinned that part of their body. **Skint** is the Scots form of *skinned*.

skirl A **skirl** is a loud shrill sound. The word is often used to describe the sound of the bagpipes: *I heard the skirl of pipes borne by the wild wind*. To **skirl** is to make a loud shrill noise such as that of the bagpipes: *The pipe music skirled and whirled*. **Skirl** is also used to refer to the sound made by food frying: *bacon and sausages skirling in the pan*.

skirlie Skirlie is a dish consisting of oatmeal and onions fried together, eaten either as a vegetable with meat dishes, or on its own with potatoes.

skite To **skite** on something, for instance ice or oil, is to slip or slide on it. To **skite** is also to travel fast and in an uncontrolled manner after bouncing off something: *My ball skited off the green and into the bunker; The hail was skitin off the pavement.* A **skite** is also a glancing blow or slap. To be **on the skite** is to be taking in part in a drunken spree: *staggering home after a night on the skite.*

skitter about To **skitter about** is to waste time doing trivial jobs rather than what is really important.

skittery or **skitterie** A **skittery** task is one which is fiddly and time-consuming.

skliff or **scliff** If someone **skliffs**, they walk without lifting their feet properly, so that their shoes scrape along the ground. A **skliff** is the sound made by someone's shoes scraping along the ground as they walk.

skoosh A variant spelling of **scoosh**.

slabber To **slabber** over something is to wet or stain it with saliva or spit, for instance when eating. In some parts of Southwest Scotland, to slabber is to work messily, particularly with something wet: *slabberin paint a' ower the bit.* **Slabber** is also a word for wet mud used in Northeast Scotland. The word is a variant of *slobber.*

slàinte mhath (pronounced *slan-ja vah*) **Slàinte mhath**, sometimes shortened to **slàinte**, is a Gaelic toast used especially when drinking whisky. It means good health.

slater A **slater** is a woodlouse (a type of small land-dwelling crustacean with a flattened segmented body).

sleekit Someone who is **sleekit** has a superficially charming and smooth manner, but is untrustworthy and sly: *sleekit-looking green eyes.*

sleuch (pronounced *slooCH*) or **sluch** (pronounced *sluCH*) To **sleuch** is to drink noisily, usually from a spoon or through a straw: *Do you have to sleuch your soup like that?*

slever (pronounced *slev-er*) To **slever** is to dribble or drool at the mouth. **Slever** (often in the plural form **slevers**) is saliva which has dribbled from someone's mouth.

slider A **slider** is a portion of ice cream between two wafers.

slitter or **slutter** A **slitter** is a person who is a messy eater or drinker. To **slitter** is to make a mess, especially by spilling or dribbling something. The word is used in Central and Southern Scotland.

slunge To **slunge** something is to rinse it superficially by pouring water over it or dipping it into water: *I'll just slunge the mugs out under the tap.*

smeddum A person who has **smeddum** has an admirable amount of determination and resourcefulness allied to common sense. This sense of the word has evolved from the earlier meaning, the most useful or powerful part of a substance, which in turn comes from the original sense, a fine powder, especially finely ground flour, which comes from the Old English *smedema.*

smiddy A **smiddy** is a blacksmith's workshop: the word is now mainly seen in the name of houses, craft shops, etc.

smirr Smirr is drizzly rain falling gently in small drops: *a smirr o rain*; *There's a bit of a smirr outside.* When it **smirrs**, there is light drizzly rain: *It's been smirring all afternoon.*

smit Any minor disease or infection is often referred to informally as **the smit**: *He's off work with the smit.* To **smit** means to infect or contaminate: *She's been smit with the 'flu.* **Smittin** means contagious or catching. The word comes from Old English, either from *smitte* a spot or *smittian* to smear.

Smokie Short for **Arbroath Smokie**.

smoor or **smore** To **smoor** is to suffocate or smother: *half-smoored by the smoke*; *sheep smoored in a snowdrift.* To **smoor** a fire is to cover it with closely-packed coal or peat last thing at night so that it continues to burn at a very low level until morning. A **smoor** is a dense enveloping cloud of smoke, mist, snow etc. The word is from the same Old English root as *smother.*

smowt or **smout** A **smowt** is a small child or undersized adult. The word is frequently encountered in the phrase *a wee smout.* A **smowt** is also a young salmon or sea trout.

snash Snash is cheeky, impudent talk: *Enough of your snash, you!*

snaw Snaw means snow. If something goes or

disappears **like snaw aff a dyke** it vanishes very quickly: _You lot vanish like snaw aff a dyke whenever there's work to be done._

sneck A **sneck** is a catch or latch on a door or gate. To **sneck** a door or gate is to fasten it with a catch or latch. Generally a **sneck** holds a door or gate shut but can be opened from either side without a key. Compare **snib**.

snell A **snell** wind is a bitingly cold one. The word comes from the Old English _snell_ quick or active.

snib A **snib** is a bolt or catch on a door or window. To **snib** a door is to lock it shut with a bolt or catch. A **snib** generally locks something securely, so that it cannot be opened from the outside, or can only be opened from the outside with a key. Compare **sneck**. The word possibly comes from the Low German _snibbe_ a beak.

snorl A **snorl** is a Northeastern word meaning an awkward situation, a scrape or predicament. It is a variant of _snarl_, as in _snarled up_.

SNP The **SNP** is the **Scottish National Party**, a political party seeking independence for Scotland.

soapy bubble Soapy bubble, often shortened to **soapy**, is Glasgow rhyming slang for trouble: _You're in deep soapy if you try that again, pal._

sodger or **sojer** (pronounced _soh-jer_) A **sodger** is a soldier. A **sodger** is also a sick or hurt child, especially one who does not complain about it.

sodie-heid (pronounced _soh-dee-heed_) A **sodie-heid** is someone who is regarded as feather-brained and unable to concentrate on anything serious for long. *Sodie* is an old Scots word, now not in common use, for soda, and a **sodie-heid** is therefore someone whose head is (metaphorically) full of bubbles.

sonsie or **sonsy** (pronounced *sonce-ee*) A **sonsie** woman or child is plump, cheerful-looking and attractive: *a sonsie lass.* The word comes from the Gaelic **sonas** meaning good fortune.

sook or **souk** A **sook** is someone who behaves sycophantically towards their superiors; a crawler or toady. To **sook in** or **sook up** is to attempt to curry favour with someone by behaving sycophantically: *You only get on here if you're prepared to sook in to the boss.* **Sook** is a Scots word for suck.

soom Soom is an old-fashioned word meaning swim: *Are ye good at the soomin?* If a place is **sooming** or is **in a soom**, it is very wet or flooded: *The kitchen was in a soom.*

soop To **soop** is to sweep. **Soop** is now mainly used as a shouted command in curling, when the person who has thrown the stone is urging their team-mates to brush the ice in the stone's path to help control its course and speed.

soor Soor means sour. Someone who has **a face that would soor milk** is very grumpy or sulky looking.

soor dook (pronounced *soor dook*) A **soor dook** is a bad-tempered or miserable looking person.

soor ploom (pronounced *soor plume*) Soor plooms are

a type of round green boiled sweet with a very tart flavour.

sooth-moother (pronounced *sooth-mooth-er*) A **sooth-moother** is a slightly derogatory Shetland name for someone with an accent from a more southerly area: *craft shops owned by sooth-moothers from Surrey and Knightsbridge.*

sore on See **sair on**.

sot Sot is a word roughly equivalent to indeed, so, or definitely, which is used, particularly by children, to contradict or deny a negative statement: *"You're feart!" "Am not!" "Are sot!"* It is a variant of *so* altered to rhyme with "not".

souch or **sough** (pronounced *sooCH*) When the wind **souchs**, it blows or howls noisily: *There's aye a gey cold wind souching down King Street.* A **souch** is the noise made by a strong wind. To **keep a calm souch** is to remain calm or quiet in a difficult situation, without panicking or getting upset or excited. The word is from the Old English *swogan* to make a rushing noise.

souk (pronounced *sook*) Another way of spelling **sook**.

soul (rhymes with *vowel*) A **soul** is any person, particularly one for whom you feel pity or affection: *the poor wee soul.*

souter or **soutar** (pronounced *soot-er*) A **souter** is a cobbler or shoemaker: like these jobs, the word is now old-fashioned. The inhabitants of Selkirk, a town formerly known for its footwear industry, are sometimes referred to as **Souters**.

Southern Uplands The **Southern Uplands** is a name sometimes given to the hilly area in the South of Scotland, which rises to over 800 metres (more than 2600 feet) in places.

spaewife (pronounced *spay-wife*) A **spaewife** is a woman who can supposedly foretell the future. The word is from the Old Norse *spá* to foretell.

spaiver or **spaver** (pronounced *spay-ver*) In some areas, particularly in the East of Scotland, the fly on a pair of trousers is called the **spaiver**: *Pull up yer spaiver, it's at half-mast.* Elsewhere it is known as the **ballop**, or simply as the fly. The word comes from the Old Scots *spair* a slit or opening in a garment.

special Special is a type of keg beer similar to **heavy** but sweeter and heavily-carbonated. It is of fairly recent invention: *Lager and special are on tap at £1.50 per pint.* It is sometimes informally shortened to **spesh**: *Ah'll have a lager; the spesh in here is bowffin.*

speir (pronounced *speer*) To **speir** is to ask or inquire. The past form is **speirt**: *They speirt if I'd seen her.*

spelk A **spelk** is the name given in some areas to a splinter of wood, especially one which has become embedded in someone's skin. Other names for this include **skelf** and **stob**.

speug (pronounced *spyug*) or **spug** A **speug** is a sparrow.

Speyside A **Speyside** whisky is one produced in

Northeast Scotland near the river Spey. This area produces many of the best known single malt whiskies. The area around the river Spey is called **Strathspey**, not **Speyside**.

Spiders Queen's Park football team is nicknamed **the Spiders**. The name refers to the alleged similarity between the narrow black and white hoops on the players' shirts and a spider's web.

spinnle-trams In some parts of Scotland **spinnle-trams** is a jocular name for skinny legs, or a person with very skinny legs. The term comes from *spinnle* spindle and *tram* a pole or post, sometimes used as a jocular name for a leg.

split-new Something which is **split-new** is brand-new: *Everything in their house is split-new and spotless.* The word refers to the clean, fresh appearance of newly cut wood.

sploonging (pronounced *sploonge-ing*) Something which is **sploonging** is soaking wet, generally with puddles of water lying on it: *Rain had been getting in through the roof, and the floor was sploonging.* The word seems to be a variant of *plunge*, with an initial *s-* added, as in *splash*.

sporran A **sporran** is a large pouch, usually made of fur, worn hanging from a belt in front of the kilt as part of men's Highland dress. The word comes from the Gaelic *sporan* purse.

sprauchle (pronounced *sprawCH-l*) or **sprachle** (pronounced *spraCH-l*) To **sprauchle** is to clamber or make one's way slowly and with difficulty: *He sprauchled up the brae.*

spug Same as **speug**.

spuilzie or **spulyie** (pronounced *spool-ee* or *spool-yee*) **Spuilzie** is an old-fashioned word meaning plunder, both as a noun and as a verb. Historically, it could mean something as serious as widespread looting and pillaging by an invading army, but if heard nowadays is more likely to refer to something relatively trivial, such as the theft of apples from somebody's garden. The word comes from the Old French *espoillier* to spoil.

spurgie (pronounced *spurg-ee*) A **spurgie** is a Northeastern word for a sparrow.

spurtle A **spurtle** is a wooden stick used for stirring porridge, rather like a wooden spoon with no bowl on it. Ultimately the word is derived from the Latin *spatula* a flat piece and the Greek *spathē* a blade, probably coming into Scots via a Scandinavian language.

square go In some parts of Scotland a **square go** is a fair one-to-one-fight between two people, without the use of weapons, usually invoked as an alternative to a large-scale brawl between two groups of people: *Words were exchanged and it ended with McNally inviting Mr Clarke for a square go in the car park.*

square sausage Square sausage, also known as **square slice** or **Lorne sausage**, is sausage meat cut in slices from a large, roughly cuboid block.

stair Scots frequently uses **stair** where English uses "stairs": *Everyone in the close has to take their turn at washing the stair.* **Up the stair** means upstairs and **doon the stair** means downstairs: *the wifie doon the stair fae me.*

stairheid (pronounced *stair-heed*) or **stairhead** A **stairheid** is a landing at the top of a flight of stairs, especially one at the top of the communal stair in a tenement. The word is often used to indicate that something takes place or is located on a stairhead: *a stairheid argument; a stairheid windae.*

stammygaster (pronounced *stam-mee-gas-ter*) A **stammygaster** is a Northeastern word meaning a shock or unpleasant surprise. To **stammygaster** someone is to give them a shock or unpleasant surprise: *He was fair stammygastered by the news.* The word is possibly a combination of the English dialect *stam* to amaze plus *aghast*.

stance A **stance** is a place where taxis wait for customers, or a bay where a bus stands in a bus station.

Standard Grade A **Standard Grade** is a qualification awarded to people who have successfully completed the lower of the two levels of **SCE** examinations. In schools it is usually taken at the end of the fourth year of secondary school (ie at the age of 15 or 16). Compare **CSYS** and **Higher**.

stane A **stane** is a stone.

stank In Central Scotland, the gutter at the side of the road is often referred to as a **stank**. In West Central Scotland, a **stank** is also a drain at the side of a road, or the grating covering such a drain. If something is said to be or to have gone **down the stank**, it is lost beyond all hope of retrieval: *That's mair money doon the stank at that bookies.*

stappit or **stappit fu** Something which is **stappit** contains as many or as much of a thing as it is possible to get in it: *Folk say that loch's stappit fu wi fish.* **Stappit** is also used to indicate that someone has eaten their fill: *Nah, no puddin for me. Ah'm stappit.*

staun (pronounced *stawn*) **Staun** means stand, both as a noun and a verb.

stave To **stave** a limb or joint is to sprain or twist it: *She had staved her wrist quite badly.* A **stave** is an injury caused by twisting or spraining a limb or joint: *You've not broken it, it's just a stave.*

stay To **stay** in a place is to have your permanent home there: *My parents stay in Balerno.*

steamie A **steamie** is an old-fashioned public laundry where people took their clothes and washed them themselves. While there are few if any still in use, the **steamie** remains part of urban folk culture in Central and Southern Scotland. To be **the talk of the steamie** is to be a person or thing much gossiped about.

steamin To be **steamin** is to be very drunk: *He came back home steamin last night again.*

Steelmen The **Steelmen** is a nickname for Motherwell football team. The town was formerly a centre of the steel industry.

steen A **steen** is a Northern word for a stone.

stewartry (pronounced *stew-art-ree*) A **stewartry** was, historically, any part of Scotland which was governed by a steward appointed by the King or Queen. **The Stewartry** is the eastern part of Galloway in Southwest Scotland. It lies between the River Nith at Dumfries and the River Cree at Newton Stewart, and has the same boundary as the former county known as **the Stewartry of Kirkcudbright** (often less formally called **Kirkcudbrightshire**), which is now administered by Dumfries and Galloway single-tier local council: *The house was gifted to the people of the Stewartry by the artist E.A. Hornel.*

stey (pronounced *stiy*) A **stey** hill or slope is steep and difficult to get up: *a stey brae.*

Stirlingshire Stirlingshire is a former inland county in Central Scotland, taking in the land on both sides of the River Forth. Most of the former county is now administered by Stirling single-tier council.

stoat or **stot** To **stoat** is to bounce: *The rain was stoatin off the pavement; She stoated the ball off the ground.*

stoater A **stoater** is something which is an outstanding or exceptional example of its kind. It is often used of a good-looking person: *See thon blonde lassie works up the stair? A right wee stoater, eh?*

stoatin or **stottin** Someone who is **stoatin** is so drunk that they have difficulty walking without staggering: *He gets stoatin fou every Friday; Don't you dare come home stoatin again tonight.*

stob A **stob** is a post, especially a fence-post. In parts of the Northeast, a **stob** is a splinter or thorn which has got stuck in someone's skin.

stookie A **stookie** is a plaster cast for a broken limb. A **stookie** is also someone who is in a situation in which they are out-of-place or feel ill-at-ease: *We just sat there like a lot of stookies.* **Stookie** is a Scots form of *stucco*, plaster of Paris, and later came to mean a plaster statue.

stoon or **stoun** (pronounced *stoon*) A **stoon** is a sharp ache, a stab of physical pain or mental anguish: *a stoon o guilt.* To **stoon** is to throb painfully. The word comes from the Old English *stund* a period of time.

stoor, stoorie Variant spellings of **stour** and **stourie**.

stooshie or **stushie** A **stooshie** is a row or uproar, usually in protest against something: *Plans to redevelop the harbour area have raised a stooshie in the town; Ach, it's no worth making a stooshie about.*

stot A variant of **stoat**.

stots and bangs To do something **by stots and bangs** is a Northeastern phrase meaning to do something now and again or intermittently: *He jist wirks in stots an bangs.*

stotter To **stotter** is to stagger or stumble: *He went stotterin off down the road.* **Stotter** is also a less common word for **stoater**.

stottin A variant of **stoatin**.

stoun (pronounced *stoon*) Another way of spelling **stoon**.

stour or **stoor** (pronounced *stoor*) **Stour** is dust, either in a cloud or a layer. An earlier sense of the word meant turmoil or conflict, and this comes from the Old French *estour* armed conflict, which is ultimately from the same source as *storm*.

stourie or **stoorie** (pronounced *stoor-ree*) A **stourie** place or thing is dusty.

stovies Stovies is a traditional dish consisting of sliced potatoes and onions stewed together, sometimes with the addition of small pieces of meat or sausage. The name is a shortening of *stoved potatoes*, from a Scots sense of *stove* meaning to cook by stewing.

stowed out (rhymes with *proud*) If a place is **stowed out**, it has more people in it than there is comfortably room for: *Let's try somewhere else, it's stowed out in here.* **Stowed out** is sometimes shortened to **stowed.**

stracht (pronounced *straCHt*) or **strecht** Stracht means straight.

stramash (pronounced *stra-mash*) A **stramash** is a disorderly commotion or argument: *Two men were arrested following a stramash in a Glasgow street.* The term is perhaps an extended form of *smash.*

strath A **strath** is a wide, flat, usually fertile valley around a river. Compare **glen**. **Strath** often forms part of a place name, such as *Strathbogie* or *Strath of Kildonan*. The word comes from the Gaelic *srath.*

Strathclyde Historically, **Strathclyde** was the name given to the ancient kingdom of the Britons which occupied much of West Central Scotland around the mouth of the river Clyde between about 450 and 1018 A.D. Its capital was at Dumbarton. **Strathclyde** is a former local government Region that occupied much of West Central Scotland and Argyll from south of Ayr to the island of Mull. The Region, Scotland's largest and most populous, is now administered by twelve single-tier local councils.

strathspey A **strathspey** is a type of dance with gliding steps similar to a reel but slower. A **strathspey** is also a piece of music in four-four time for, or in the style of music for, this dance. The dance apparently originated in the area of *Strathspey* in Northeast Scotland.

stravaig (pronounced *stra-vague*) To **stravaig** is to wander or roam aimlessly. A **stravaig** is a long, aimless ramble or journey. The word comes via the obsolete Scots *extravage* from the Latin *vagārī* to wander.

strecht (pronounced *streCHt*) A variant of **stracht**.

stretcher or **streetcher** A **stretcher** is a long pole with a notch in one end of it, which is used as a prop to support the middle of a clothes line.

stroupach (pronounced *stroop-aCH*) A **stroupach** is a name given to a drink of tea in the far North of Scotland. The word comes from *stroup*, the mouth or spout of a kettle, pump, etc, plus the diminutive ending *-ach*.

stue (pronounced *stew*) **Stue** is a Northeastern word for dust, either in a cloud or a layer. Elsewhere the word **stour** is generally used instead.

stushie (rhymes with *pushy*) Another spelling of **stooshie**.

sugarallie (pronounced *shoo-gar-al-lee*) or **sugarollie** (pronounced *shoo-gar-ol-lee*) Sugarallie is an old-fashioned name for liquorice. **Sugarallie water** is a soft drink which children used to make by dissolving pieces of liquorice in water. It is still used as a description of any drink that is too weak or too sweet for the drinker's taste: *Yon Liebfraumilch's just sugarallie water.* The word comes from *sugar* plus *alicreesh*, an old name for liquorice.

sumph (pronounced *sumf*) A sumph is a stupid, slow-witted person, who is regarded as not being much good at anything: *Ye muckle sumph!*

supper In a fish-and-chip shop, a **supper** consists of an item of food specified served with chips: *a fish supper; a pakora supper.*

Sutherland Sutherland is an area and former county in the extreme Northwest of Scotland. It is now administered by Highland single-tier local council.

swack Swack is a North of Scotland word which means fit and supple: *I'm no so swack as I used to be.* It comes from the Flemish *zwak* or Middle Dutch *swac*, both of which mean lithe.

swally or **swallie** (rhymes with *rally*) A swally is a drink of alcohol, or a period of time spent drinking alcohol: *Fancy a quick swally after work?* To **swally** something is to swallow it: *Swally the rest of your tea and we'll go.*

swatch (rhymes with *catch*) A swatch at something is a look at it: *Gies a swatch at the paper when you're finished wi it.*

sweetie A **sweetie** is a piece of confectionery, a sweet. To **work for sweeties** is to be exceptionally badly paid: *Many directors pay themselves huge salaries while expecting their employees to work for sweeties.*

sweetiewife A **sweetiewife** is a person, especially a man, who is very gossipy. This sense of the word has developed from the earlier meaning, a woman who sells sweets.

sweir (pronounced *sweer*) To be **sweir** to do something is to be unwilling or reluctant to do it. The word comes from the Old Northumbrian *swær* meaning lazy.

swick To **swick** is to cheat or swindle: *Ye were swickit there.* A **swick** is a swindle or swindler. The word, which now seems to be most common in the Northeast, comes from the Old English *swican* to cheat.

swither To **swither** is to be unable to decide or choose between things or courses of action: *The board is still swithering about investing many millions in a new ground or renovating the current stadium.* A **swither** is a state of indecision: *I'm in a bit of a swither about what to wear.*

syboes (pronounced *siy-beez*) **Syboes** are spring onions. The word is from the French *ciboule*, which in turn comes from the Latin *cēpola* a small onion.

synd or **syne** (pronounced *sign*) To **synd** something is to rinse it or wash it superficially: *Synd oot thae dishes.* A **synd** is a rinse or superficial wash.

syne (pronounced *sign*) **Syne** means since or ago: *a year* *syne.* It can also mean thereupon or then: *Syne in comes ma mither.* Both these senses are fairly old fashioned in most of Scotland, and the word is now mainly heard in the phrase **auld lang syne**, meaning the days of long ago, and even this is best known as the title of a song.

syver (pronounced *sigh-ver*) A **syver** is a drain in a road, or the grating covering such a drain.

tablet Tablet is a type of sweet like a firmer version of fudge, made from butter, sugar, and sometimes condensed milk. It is presumably so called because it is usually made in a flat oblong block before being broken into pieces.

tacket A tacket is a hobnail or segg on the sole of a boot or shoe.

tackety Tackety boots or shoes have hobnails or studs in their soles: *a decent pair of tackety boots with steel toecaps.*

tae (pronounced *tay*) ① Tae means to: *We've goat wur reputations tae think aboot; Dinnae listen tae that ignorant bastard; He took hissel aff tae England.* ② Tae also means too, chiefly in the sense of "as well": *It's wonderful how that woman copes wi that child. An her a widow, tae!* Compare **ower**. ③ A tae is a toe.

tait A tait is a small piece or amount of something: *a wee tait of sugar.* The word is probably of Scandinavian origin: compare *tæta*, the Icelandic word for a shred.

tak To tak means to take: *I'll tak ye to the hotel.*

take To **take your hand off someone's face** or **jaw** is to slap or smack them on the head. The phrase is generally used as a parent's threat to a naughty child: *I'll take my hand off your face if you do that again, my lad!*; *He claimed he didn't assault his wife, he just "took a hand off her jaw"*. It is, of course, the hand being put rapidly onto the face that is to be feared, not its being removed.

tak tent To **tak tent** of something is to pay heed to it, particularly when it is something that can be interpreted as a warning to take care.

Tally or **Tallie** **Tally** is an informal, slightly old-fashioned word meaning Italian: *real Tally ice-cream*.

tammy A **tammy** is a round, flat brimless woollen cap rather like a beret, sometimes with a bobble on the top of it. The name is a shortening of *Tam o' Shanter* (see next entry).

Tam o' Shanter A **Tam o' Shanter** is a man's flat round brimless woollen cap with a bobble on the top of it. It is named after the hero of Burns' poem *Tam o' Shanter*.

Tangerines Dundee United football team is nicknamed **the Tangerines**. The term comes from the orange colour of the shirts in the team's home strip.

tangle The word **tangle** refers to any of various types of brown seaweed with long broad fronds which grow between the high and low water marks: *They spent the morning breaking tangles on the shore*.

tap The **tap** of something is its top: *at the tap o the brae*.

tapsalteerie (pronounced *tap-sl-tea-ree*) Something

which is **tapsalteerie** is upside-down. **Tapsalteerie** also
means untidy and chaotic, or in an untidy and chaotic
manner: *Dirty clothes were scattered tapsalteerie around the room.*
The word is a Scottish form of *topsy-turvy*.

tarry-fingert (pronounced *tar-ree-fing-ert*) Someone
who is **tarry-fingert** has a tendency to steal things: a
chiefly Northeastern word.

tartan A **tartan** is a distinctive pattern of coloured
lines and bands which cross each other at right angles.
They originated in the Highlands. Many tartans are
nowadays associated with particular **clans**, although
there is little convincing historical evidence for this. The
earliest tartans seem to have been coloured with
whatever natural dyes were available in an area, and
hence were local tartans rather than clan tartans,
although since most people in an area belonged to the
same clan this is perhaps rather a fine distinction.
Following the failure of the 1745 Jacobite Rebellion,
the wearing of tartan was banned as part of a
concentrated effort to destroy the traditional Highland
way of life. Tartan re-emerged in the early 19th-century
Romantic enthusiasm for all things Scottish, but many
of the allegedly traditional designs published in books
such as the Sobieski Stuarts' "Vestiarium Scoticum" are
in fact spurious. **Tartan** cloth, or a **tartan** garment, is
woven with such a pattern in it: *a tartan rug.* **Tartan** is
also disparagingly used to indicate that something is
Scottish in an exaggerated, self-conscious, or bigotedly
nationalistic way (but see also **Tartan Army**): *Labour and*

*the SNP continue to accuse each other of being "Tartan Tories";
Tartan terrorists have issued death threats against a number of
English residents.*

Tartan Army The supporters who follow Scotland's
national football team to matches overseas are
affectionately nicknamed the Tartan Army: *The Tartan
Army turned out in low numbers for the World Cup qualifying
campaign.*

tartanry Tartanry is a derogatory term for the
excessive use of tartan and other Scottish imagery to
produce a distorted sentimental view of Scotland and
its history: *a popular culture based on tartanry, Highland Games,
and sentimentality.*

tassie A tassie is a cup or goblet. Nowadays the word
is hardly ever used except in the name of various sports
trophies: *The draw for next month's Silver Tassie competition will
be made on Wednesday.* The word comes from the Old
French *tasse* a cup.

tattie (pronounced *tat-ee* or *tot-ee*) A tattie is a potato:
mince and tatties; tattie soup. The term is a shortened altered
form of **potato**.

tattie-bogle (pronounced *boh-gl*) A tattie-bogle is a
name for a scarecrow used throughout Scotland with the
exception of the Northeast.

tattie-boodie A tattie-boodie is a Northeastern name
for a scarecrow.

tattie holidays The tattie holidays is the name given

in many rural areas to the week or so of school holidays in October, which was originally given to allow children to help with the potato harvest.

tattie howkin Tattie howkin is the harvesting of potatoes by digging them out of the ground. See **howk**.

tattie-peelin (pronounced *tat-tee-peel-in*) In some parts of Central Scotland, something which is regarded as affectedly posh or pretentious can be described as **tattie-peelin**. The term is most often used of an accent.

tattie scone Same as a **potato scone**.

tawse (rhymes with *pause*) A **tawse** is a leather strap with two or more thongs at one end with which school children were formerly hit as a punishment. Its use is now illegal: *The tawse was often administered stupidly and sadistically.*

Tayside Tayside is a former local government Region in Eastern Central Scotland that occupied the area around the River Tay and that north of the Firth of Tay as far as Montrose. It is now administered by three single-tier local councils: Perthshire and Kinross, Angus, and the City of Dundee.

tea or **high tea** The main evening meal, usually eaten at about five or six in the evening, is known as **tea**: *We're having steak for tea.* It traditionally consists of one main course plus bread, cakes, and the like. In the Glasgow area, to say that **someone's tea is out** is to indicate that they are about to get into trouble: *Your tea's oot if the boss finds ye've been pochling the time sheet.*

tea jenny See **jenny**.

Teddy Bears The **Teddy Bears** is one of the nicknames of Rangers football team. It is rhyming slang for *Gers*, the broad Glaswegian pronunciation of "bear" being "berr".

teem To **teem** something is to empty it: *Teem your cup and then we can go.* Something which is **teem** is empty.

tee-name In some parts of the Northeast, if a person has been given a nickname to distinguish them from other people with the same or a similar name, this is known as a **tee-name**. The word is a local form of *to-name*, a name used to address someone.

Teerie A **Teerie** is a person from Hawick. The term comes from the song traditionally sung as part of the Hawick Common Riding: "*Teribus* and Teriodin, We will up and Ride the Common". "Teribus and Teriodin" is most likely a nonsense phrase imitative of the sound of military drumming.

telling To **take a telling** is to take heed of a warning or scolding: the phrase is usually used of someone who **wouldn't** or **won't take a telling**: *I told you you'd hurt yourself doing it like that, but you wouldn't take a telling, would you?*

telt Telt is a broad Scots form of *told*: *Ah've no seen it, Ah telt ye.*

term-day A **term-day** is one of the four days on which certain payments, for instance rents or interest, become due, and on which, formerly, annual contracts of employment and leases were signed. The four **term-days** are **Candlemas**, **Whitsunday**, **Lammas** and **Martinmas**.

terr In Central Scotland, a **terr** is any event or period of time during which people have great fun: *You missed yoursel last night; we'd a rerr terr.*

teuch (pronounced *chooCH* or *chuCH*) Food which is **teuch** is tough and hard to chew: *This steak's a bit teuch.*

teuchat (pronounced *chooCH-it*) A **teuchat** is the name given in some Eastern parts of Scotland to the bird more generally known as a **peewit** or lapwing. The name is imitative of the bird's call.

teuchter (pronounced *chooCH-ter*) A **teuchter** is a Lowland name for a Highlander, especially a Gaelic-speaking one. While not openly derogatory, it has overtones which suggest that the speaker considers all Highlanders to be unsophisticated peasants and does not indicate any great respect for Highland ways and traditions: *They put up bilingual street signs in Airdrie so that the teuchters down for the Mod could find their way around.* In the North **teuchter** is used more generally to refer to a person from any rural area: *The Inverness people used to call us teuchters and make fun of our Island accents.* **Teuchter** can also be used as an adjective to indicate that a thing or place is typical of, or popular with, people from the Highlands: *Shinty's a teuchter game, isn't it?; a pub frequented by Glasgow's teuchter community.* Various etymologies have been suggested – that it comes from Gaelic *tuath* meaning country people or the north; that it is from

Gaelic *deoch* a drink, particularly of whisky; or that it is from the Scots *teuch* tough – but the word's origin remains unclear.

thae (pronounced *they*) **Thae** means those: *Post thae letters for me, will ye?*

the A number of ways of using **the** are characteristically Scottish. It is often used with periods of time such as "day" or "night" instead of "this" or "to-": *the day; the nicht.* **The** is also sometimes used instead of a possessive pronoun such as "my" or "your": *I got mud all over the good suit; I'm taking the wee brother to the game.* **The** is often used where it would be omitted in English, for instance before the names of institutions, activities, or illnesses: *Has Mary started at the school yet?; She's keen on the dancing; a dose of the flu.* It is also traditionally used by locals before the name of certain towns, villages, and areas of towns: *the Langholm; the Raploch; the Longman; the Paisley Road.*

thegither (pronounced *the-giTH-er*) **Thegither** means together: *Freedom and whisky gang thegither.*

thirled To be **thirled** to something is to be bound to it by obligation, duty or habit: *Scottish public sector workers are thirled to the British state which pays their wages.* The word comes from the same Old English root as *thrall.*

this In the Glasgow area, the expression **this is me** is used to indicate that the speaker is in a particular state, and often has been for some considerable time: *This is me waitin three weeks to get the video fixed.*

thistle The **thistle** is the national emblem of Scotland, used for instance as a badge on the jerseys of the Scottish national rugby team. The **Order of the Thistle** is the highest Scottish order of knighthood, consisting of the King or Queen plus sixteen Knights.

thocht (pronounced *thoCHt*) **Thocht** means thought, both as a verb and as a noun: *We thocht we'd better mak a start; It was jist a thocht.*

thole To **thole** something is to endure, tolerate or put up with it, especially because there is no alternative: *Scotland have had to thole a major turnover in personnel between matches; I canna thole yon man.* The word, which is also used in the North of England, is of Old English origin, and is related to the Latin *tollere* to bear up.

thon (pronounced *THon*) **Thon** means that or those: *thon guy who works at the garage; What do ye cry thon Greek thingies again?* It is a combination of *that* and *yon.*

thrang **Thrang** means busy, both in the sense of crowded with people and the sense fully occupied doing something: *streets thrang with shoppers; I'm ower thrang to help.* The word is a variant of *throng.*

thrapple The **thrapple** is the throat or windpipe. The term possibly comes from the Old English *throtbolla* the Adam's apple, from *throte* throat plus *bolla* boll.

thraw In the East of Scotland, to **thraw** a joint or limb is to twist or sprain it: *I've thrawed my ankle.* The word is a Scots form of *throw.*

thrawn To be **thrawn** is to be awkward and obstinate and take delight in being difficult and uncooperative: *a wonderfully thrawn old man of 75; a thrawn inability to agree about anything important.*

throw A **throw** is a sequence of ornamental grace-notes of a type common in bagpipe music.

thunder-plump A **thunder-plump** is a sudden thundery shower of rain. See also **plump**.

ticht (pronounced *tiCHt*) **Ticht** means tight.

ticket A **ticket** is a Glasgow term for any person, especially one of a stated appearance or reputation: *a right hard ticket.*

tig Tig is a children's game in which one player chases and tries to catch the others by touching one of them. In the most simple version of the game, known simply as **tig**, the person who has been caught then becomes the chaser. There are many slightly more complicated variants, such as **high tig** in which a player cannot be caught if no part of their body is touching the ground, and **chain tig** in which a player who is caught must join hands with the catcher and the game ends with a long chain of players holding hands and trying to catch the one player who is still free. To **tig** someone is to catch someone playing this game by touching them.

til or **till Til** means to or towards: *He had been a good son til them; We gaed til the kirk.* Except in some parts of the Far North, **til** is not normally used as part of the infinitive: *tae gang til the kirk.*

Tim A **Tim** is a West Central Scottish nickname for a Roman Catholic: *Are you a Billy or a Tim?*

time about (pronounced *time a-bout*) If people do something **time about**, they do it alternately or turn and turn about: *We drove time about.*

timeous (pronounced *time-us*) Something which is **timeous** is in good time and sufficiently early to be acted on or taken heed of: *a timeous warning.*

tink A **tink** is someone who moves from place to place buying and selling things and doing casual work, a Traveller: *It's just some tinks out hunting rabbits.* **Tink** is also used as a derogatory name for anyone whose behaviour or speech is regarded as unacceptably quarrelsome or abusive. A mischievous and cheeky young child can also be referred to as a **tink**.

tinker In Scotland, a **tinker** is a Gypsy or any other Traveller who moves from place to place buying and selling things and doing casual work, not just a travelling mender of pots and pans.

tinkler A **tinkler** is the same as a **tinker**: *the distinctive speech of the tinklers.* In some parts of Scotland, **tinkler** is also used as a derogatory name for any person whose behaviour or speech is unacceptably coarse.

tint If something has been **tint**, it has been lost. The word is still used in the Northeast, but is considered old-fashioned elsewhere. The nineteenth-century hanging judge Lord Braxfield once criticized someone's anglified accent by proclaiming that *the laddie has clean tint* *his Scotch, and found nae English.* **Tint** is the past of *tine* to lose.

tirl To **tirl** something is to knock on or rattle it. One version of the nursery rhyme "Wee Willie Winkie" has him *tirlin on the windae, cryin through the lock.*

tolbooth (pronounced *toll-booth*) A **tolbooth** is a building formerly used as a town hall and prison and also sometimes as a tax office. The buildings still exist in many towns, and are put to a variety of modern-day uses: *Kirkcudbright's historic Tolbooth was recently converted to an arts centre.* It is so called because it was originally a *booth* or stall where *tolls* and taxes were collected.

toon A **toon** is a town: *I'll go into the toon to meet him.*

toorie A **toorie** is a round bobble or pompom on a hat. A **toorie** or **toorie bunnet** is any of various hats or caps with a bobble on it, especially a knitted bobble-hat resembling a tea-cosy. The term is a diminutive of *toor*, the Scots form of *tower*.

torn-faced (pronounced *torn-faced*) Someone who is **torn-faced** has a bad-tempered or grumpy expression: a term most common in Central Scotland: *What's that torn-faced old bitch on about now?*

totie (pronounced *tote-ee*) or **tottie** (pronounced *tot-ee*) Something which is **totie** is very small: *totie wee new potatoes.* The word comes from *tot* a small child, which was originally Scots.

tottie or **totty** (pronounced *tot-ee*) West Central Scottish variants of **tattie**.

toun (pronounced *toon*) An old-fashioned variant of **toon**: *St John's Toun of Perth*. See also **farm-toun**.

tousie (rhymes with *choosy*) **Tousie** hair is tangled and untidy: *a tousie-heided wean*. The word comes from the same Germanic root as **tousle**.

tow (rhymes with *now*) **Tow** is any sort of rope, cord, or string. The Eastern Scottish saying **let the tow gang wi the bucket** means that one must accept that a situation cannot be improved and all there is to do is accept one's losses.

Town House The **Town House** is the name given to the town hall or council offices in some Scottish towns and cities, notably Aberdeen, Inverness and Kirkcaldy.

towsie (rhymes with *drowsy*) A **towsie** game in a sport such as football or rugby is one in which there is little flowing play and many petty (or not-so-petty) fouls: *It was a towsie relegation battle with no goals but plenty of bookings.*

Trades In some places, including Aberdeen, Dundee and Edinburgh, the annual July holiday period for manual workers, factory workers, etc is known as **the Trades Holidays**, **the Trades Fortnight**, or simply **the Trades**. In other parts of Scotland such a holiday is known as a **Fair**.

trauchle (pronounced *trawCH-l*) or **trachle** (pronounced *traCH-l*) **Trauchle** is work or a task which is tiring, monotonous, and takes a long time to complete: *It took years of hard trauchle before he saw any success.* To **trauchle** is to walk or work slowly and wearily: *She* *trauchled up the brae with her bags of messages; trauchling away at a job he hated.* Someone who is **trauchled** is exhausted by long hard work. The word seems to be of Dutch origin.

trews Trews are close-fitting trousers of the type worn as part of the formal uniform of certain Scottish regiments. The word comes from the Gaelic *triubhas* trews or trousers.

tron In an old Scottish town, the **tron** was the place or building at which the official public weighing machine for checking the weight of goods was kept. The word is still used in place names such as *the Tron Kirk* and *Trongate*. It is ultimately derived from the Greek *trutanē* a balance or set of scales.

Trossachs (pronounced *tross-aks*) Strictly speaking, the **Trossachs** is a narrow wooded valley in the north of Central Scotland between Loch Katrine and Loch Achray. In popular usage, however, the term is used to cover the area extending north from Loch Ard and Aberfoyle to Lochs Katrine, Achray, and Vennachar.

tube A **tube** is a Glaswegian term for a fool or idiot: *What does that tube think he's playing at?*

tumble To **take a tumble to oneself** is to get a grip on oneself and buck up one's ideas, for instance by working harder or paying more attention: *You'd better take a tumble to yourself if you want to go on working here.*

tummle (pronounced *tum-ml*) Tummle is a Scots form of tumble. To **tummle one's wilkies** (in West Central Scotland) or **tummle the cat** (in the Northeast) is to turn a somersault or somersaults. "Wilkies" is a contraction of *wild cats*; both versions of the phrase refer to a cat's ability to twist and turn.

tumshie (pronounced *tum-shee*) A **tumshie** is a Central and Southern Scottish word for a turnip.

turn To **turn** is to convert from Catholicism to Presbyterianism or vice-versa: *Her parents didn't want us to get married unless I agreed to turn.*

twa (pronounced *twaw* or *twah*) or **twae** (pronounced *tway*) **Twa** means two: *twa corbies; his ain twae sons.*

tyauve (pronounced *chawv*) A variant spelling of **chauve**.

unco (pronounced *ung-ka*) **Unco** means very or extremely: *The island has a whisky trail for the unco drouthy.* The phrase **unco guid** is used to describe those who are excessively religious, self-righteous, or narrow-minded. One of Burns's most well-known poems is the `Address to the Unco Guid', an attack on the rigidly righteous: *Is Gaeldom populated exclusively by drunks and the unco guid?* **Unco** is also used to mean strange or unfamiliar: *an unco sicht.* The word is a Scottish variant of *uncouth.*

Up-Helly-Aa (pronounced *up-hell-ee-ah*) **Up-Helly-Aa** is an annual festival held in Lerwick in Shetland on the last Tuesday of January. The last hundred years has seen it evolve from a fire festival honouring the sun during the winter solstice into a celebration of Shetland's Norse heritage. The culmination of the modern-day festival consists of a torch-lit procession of locals dressed in Viking costumes who then throw their torches into a Viking long ship newly built by the islanders. The word is from *up* finished and *haliday* a Scots form of holiday, as the celebration comes at the end of the Yule holiday.

uplift (pronounced *up-lift*) To **uplift** is to pick up, collect, or take possession of something: *They had instructed their hauliers not to uplift grain if there was any doubt about where it had been stored; He came round to uplift the rent.*

upset price The **upset price** of an item at an auction in Scotland is the minimum price at which the owner is willing to sell. The English equivalent is reserve price.

ur (rhymes with *fur*) In Glasgow and West Central Scotland, **ur** is a spoken form of are: *Ur youse no ready yet?*

ùrlar (pronounced *oor-lar*) In bagpipe music an **ùrlar** is the basic tune around which a **pibroch** is based. The word is Gaelic and means floor.

urnae (rhymes with *journey*) In Glasgow and West Central Scotland, **urnae** is a spoken form of am not: *Am urnae gaun tae the dancin the night.*

vatted malt A **vatted malt** is a type of whisky made by mixing a variety of single malts. It is at a level between a blend and a single malt in terms of quality and price.

vennel A **vennel** is a lane or alley: *the vennels of Edinburgh's Old Town*. The term is often found in street names such as *Friars Vennel* or *South Vennel*. The word comes from the French *venelle*.

In Orkney and Shetland a **voe** is a small bay or narrow creek: *The Isle of Balta all but fills the mouth of the voe*. The word often forms part of place names, such as *Sullom Voe* or *Sandsound Voe*. The word comes from Old Norse.

h (rhymes with *batch*) A **vratch** is a Northeastern word meaning a despicable or pitiable person. The word is a local form of *wretch*.

wa (pronounced *waw* or *wah*) A **wa** is a wall: *stoatin a ba aff the wa.*

wabbit (rhymes with *rabbit*) To be **wabbit** is to be tired, run down, and lacking in energy: *I think I'll have an early night; I'm feeling a bit wabbit.*

wallie or **wally** (rhymes with *alley*) Something which is **wallie** is made of porcelain or glazed china. A **wallie dug** is a china dog, usually one of a pair, which is used as an ornament on shelves and mantelpieces. In the Glasgow area, a **wallie close** is a **close**, especially one in a late 19th or early 20th century tenement, which is lined with china tiles. The more upmarket the building originally was, the more tiles there are, and the more elaborately they are decorated: *tiled walls that convey the impression of visiting one's respectable uncle in a West End wally close.* These senses have developed over the years from earlier ones. Originally, **wallie** meant fine or admirable, and then a sense meaning pleasant to look at emerged (the poet Allan Ramsay wrote of *a winsome lass and waly*). From this it came to mean ornamental, and finally, because so many ornaments were made of china or porcelain, the present meaning appeared.

wallies (rhymes with *alleys*) **Wallies** are false teeth or dentures: *Ah cannae eat an aipple since Ah got these wallies.*

wan (rhymes with *man*) **Wan** is a chiefly West Central and Southwestern word for one: *It's the wan wi the photie oan it; The odds are ten tae wan.*

wance (rhymes with *dance*) **Wance** is a word for once, used mainly in West Central Scotland: *He had wan wance.*

wanchancy (pronounced *wann-chance-ee*) **Wanchancy** is a literary word meaning unfortunate or unlucky. It comes from **wan-** meaning un- plus **chancy** lucky.

warmer (pronounced *warrm-er* or *warm-er*) A **warmer** is an exceptionally annoying or disgusting person: *Is she away hame an left you tae finish up? Oh, she's a warmer, that yin!*

warrant sale A **warrant sale** is a forced sale of a debtor's property in order to pay off debts: *a poinding of goods at his home in preparation for a warrant sale.* Certain essential goods, such as bedding, cookers, and furniture cannot be sold in a warrant sale.

Warriors Stenhousemuir football team are nicknamed **the Warriors.**

warsle (rhymes with *parcel*) To **warsle** is, literally, to wrestle, but nowadays the word is generally used, most frequently in the Northeast, to mean struggling through life or getting by with difficulty: *"Foo're ye deein?" "Och, warslin on."*

wash In whisky-making, the **wash** is the beer-like liquid which is produced by the fermentation of the yeast and barley mixture and is then distilled to produce the whisky.

washback A **washback** is a large vat used in whisky-making in which yeast is added to the water and grain mixture and the liquid is then left to ferment and produce the **wash**. (A *back* is a large tub or vat).

Wasps Alloa Athletic football team are nicknamed **the Wasps** because of the yellow and black colours of their traditional strip.

waste To **waste** something is to spoil or damage it by ill-use: *He's wastit his good trainers playing fitba*. To **waste** a child is to spoil it by giving in to all its demands: *Your Grampa's got you wastit wi thae sweeties, hasn't he?*

watter (rhymes with *matter*) **Watter** is water. See also **doon the watter**.

waulk (pronounced *walk*) To **waulk** cloth is to full it, that is, to make it heavier and more compact by a process of soaking, rhythmic beating or pounding, and shrinking.

waulking song A **waulking song** is a type of rhythmic call-and-response folk song originally sung by Hebridean women while **waulking** cloth by hand: *It was an entertaining set that included slow airs, frisky hornpipes, and waulking songs.*

wean (rhymes with *pain*) A **wean** is a child, particularly a young one: *Try that if you have four weans and a fat lazy husband; an exchange scheme involving local weans and some pupils from Germany.* The word, which is used mainly in West Central Scotland, is a contraction of *wee ane* little one.

wecht (pronounced *weCHt*) Wecht means weight.

wee Wee means small or little: *a wee dram; There's just one wee problem; I suppose I'm a wee bit biased.* **Wee** can also mean young, or at least younger than the speaker or other person mentioned: *stories my grannie told me when I was wee; If you think he's tall you should see his wee brother.* The comparative and superlative can be either **wee-er** and **wee-est** or **weer** and **weest**: *She was wee-er than many of the teenagers she taught; the weest boy in the class.* A **wee** is a short period of time: *Bide a wee.* The word comes from the Old English *wǣg* a weight.

Weedgie (pronounced *wee-jee*) A **Weedgie** is a derogatory Edinburgh name for a person from Glasgow: *Why build a new stadium on the outskirts where it will be easier for Weedgies to get to than the club's own supporters?* The term, which seems to be of recent origin, is a shortening of *Glaswegian.*

Wee Free A **Wee Free** is an informal, slightly derogatory, nickname for a member of the **Free Church of Scotland**, which is regarded by many as one of the last redoubts of traditional puritanism and sabbatarianism: *Call me a hung-up, sour-pussed, grim Wee Free if you like.* They are known as "Wee" Frees because the current Free Church is descended from the minority group which broke away to maintain its independence when the original Free Church merged with the United Presbyterian Church in 1900. The Free Kirk is most active in the West Highlands and the Hebrides.

wee heavy A **wee heavy** is a type of strong beer or barley wine traditionally served in a small measure.

weel Weel means well: *He's no awfy weel; He's no weel aff.*

weel-kent (pronounced *weel-kent*) Someone or something which is **weel-kent** is well known or familiar: *They are weel-kent names to Scotland's real ale drinkers.*

wee man In the name o the wee man! is an expression of surprise or outrage The **wee man** in question is the devil.

weemen (pronounced *weem-in*) or **weemenfolk** Weemen are women: *The weemenfolk seem to be taking over.*

Wee Rangers Berwick Rangers football team are nicknamed **the Wee Rangers**. The name refers to the fact that they are less successful and prosperous than Glasgow Rangers.

well-fired A **well-fired** roll, scone, etc. is one which has been baked for a longer time than usual so that the top crust is dark brown or black and crisp in texture.

wellied Someone who is **wellied** is drunk.

well on (pronounced *well on*) Someone who is **well on** is drunk and in the process of getting drunker: *He was already well on when I got to the pub.*

wersh Food or drink which is **wersh** does not taste very nice. However, there are two contradictory things that might be wrong with it. The earlier sense of **wersh** means bland and lacking in flavour or seasoning, and in particular cooked without enough salt: *Soup made with water rather than stock can be gey wersh.* While this meaning remains in general use, a second sense, meaning harsh, sour, or bitter, has emerged: *The strawberries were still wersh and under-ripe.* There seems to be no clear-cut regional distinction between the senses. **Wersh** probably comes from the Middle English *werische* insipid or sickly.

wester The **wester** part of an area is the part of it which is furthest west. The word is generally used in place names such as *Wester Ross* or *Wester Hailes.*

Western Isles The **Western Isles** is another name for the Hebrides. The name is frequently used to refer to the Outer Hebrides alone. Many parts of the Western Isles, particularly the Outer Hebrides, still use Gaelic as an everyday language, and the Outer Hebrides are officially bilingual, with Gaelic and English both used on road signs etc.

West Lothian West Lothian is a former county in central Scotland, at the Southwestern end of the Firth of Forth. It is now the name of a single-tier local council administering much the same area as the old county.

wha (pronounced *whaw*) or **whae** (pronounced *whay*) **Wha** means who: *Here's tae us, wha's like us?; Listen tae whae's talkin!*

what way What way means how: *What way dae ye do it?* It can also mean why: *What way can I no go?*

whaup (pronounced *whawp*) A **whaup** is a Scots name for a curlew. The word is related to the Old English *huilpe*, a name for some type of sea-bird, and is ultimately imitative of the bird's cry.

whaur (pronounced *whawr*) **Whaur** means where: *It's whaur the burn runs by the kirk; Whaur's yer Wullie Shakespeare noo?*

wheech (pronounced *wheeCH*) To **wheech** is to move quickly: *He went wheeching down the hill on his bike.* To **wheech** something is to move or remove it quickly and suddenly: *The barman tried to wheech my pint away before I'd finished.* A **wheech** is a sudden quick movement. The word is an attempt to imitate the sound of something moving rapidly through the air.

wheen A **wheen** is an indeterminate but reasonably large number or quantity: *There's still a wheen of work to do; a wheen parcels.*

wheesht or **wheesh** "Wheesht!" is an interjection meaning "Be quiet!" or "Shut up!" To **wheesht** someone is to tell them to be quiet: *parents wheeshting their children.* To **haud one's wheesht** is to be quiet: *If you two would just haud your wheesht we might hear what's going on.*

whigmaleerie (pronounced *whig-ma-leer-ee*) A **whigmaleerie** is a decoration, trinket, or ornament: *the whigmaleeries and curlie-wurlies of statuettes which adorn the monument.*

whisky **Whisky** is an alcoholic spirit made by distilling fermented cereals, especially malted barley. There are two types of whisky, **malt whisky** which is made purely from malted barley, and **grain whisky**, which can use other cereals, not necessarily malted. The **whisky** is made by mixing the malt or other grains with water and yeast, allowing this to ferment to produce a liquid rather like beer, which is then distilled. The final product must mature for at least three years before it can legally be sold. Scotch **whisky**, unlike Irish and U.S. whiskey, is always spelled without an "e". The name comes from the Gaelic *uisge beatha* the water of life.

whit Whit means what: *Whit's she up tae?; Dae whit ye're tellt!*

white pudding A **white pudding** is a type of sausage which is filled with oatmeal flavoured with suet, onions, salt, and pepper: *a white pudding supper.*

Whitsunday Whitsunday is one of the four Scottish term-days (or quarter days), on May 15th.

whitterick (pronounced *whit-er-ik*) A **whitterick** is a Central and Southern Scottish name for a weasel or stoat. The word is a variant of *whitrat*, which originally meant white rat.

wi Wi means with: *Dae whit ye like wi them; He's an awfy man wi a drink in him.*

widdershins or **withershins** To move **widdershins** is to move anti-clockwise or in a direction opposite to the course of the sun. **Widdershins** is often regarded as the opposite way from normal, and among the superstitious to do something **widdershins** is thought to bring bad luck: *He made a circling motion widdershins in the air.* The opposite of this is **deasil**. The term comes from a Middle High German word meaning opposite course, from *wider* against plus *sin* course.

widna (pronounced *wid-na*) or **widnae** (pronounced *wid-nee*) **Widna** means wouldn't: *I widnae say that.*

wifie (pronounced *wife-ee*) A **wifie** is a woman, particularly a middle-aged one: *a host of schoolchildren and assorted wifies.*

Wigtownshire (pronounced *wig-ten-sher* or *wig-ten-shire*) **Wigtownshire** is a former county in the Southwestern corner of Scotland, which borders on the Irish Sea and the Solway Firth and forms the more westerly part of Galloway. It is now administered by Dumfries and Galloway single-tier local council. Locally it is often referred to simply as **the Shire**.

wild hyacinth The **wild hyacinth** is the traditional Scots name for the flower known in England as the bluebell. **Bluebell** traditionally refers to a different flower in Scotland.

wilkies Tummle one's wilkies. See **tummle**.

winch (pronounced *winsh*) To **winch** is to be romantically involved with someone: *He said he'd been winchin but had chucked her.* To **winch** is also to kiss and cuddle, to snog: *Her mum caught us winching on the sofa.* Although **winching** can be done by either sex, the word was originally a variant of **wench**.

windae (pronounced *windy*) A **windae** is a window: *A bird hut the windae.*

winna (pronounced *win-na*) **Winna** means will not or won't: *You winna listen.*

wise (rhymes with *nice*) Someone who is **no wise** is

lacking in common sense: *He's only just met the lassie but he gies her a len o his motor? The boy's no wise.*

wish To **wish** something is to want it. In Scots it is possible simply to "wish" something rather than to "wish for" it. This usage is particularly common among staff in shops and restaurants: *Do you wish coffee?*

withershins (pronounced *wiTH-er-shinz*) Same as **widdershins**.

workie (rhymes with *murky*) A **workie** is a Glaswegian term for a workman: *sitting in all day waiting for the workies to come.*

wrang (pronounced *rang*) **Wrang** means wrong: *the wrang yin*; *That's where we've been gaun wrang.*

Writer to the Signet A **Writer to the Signet** is a member of a society of solicitors who are the only ones allowed to prepare writs on behalf of the Crown. It is often abbreviated to **W.S.** in the names of law firms. A *writer* is an old word for a solicitor.

wulk A **wulk** is a whelk or periwinkle. To be **fou as a wulk** is to be drunk.

wurnae (rhymes with *journey*) **Wurnae** means weren't: *We wurnae even there.*

wyle To **wyle** is a Northeastern word meaning to choose. A **wyle** is a choice or selection. **The wyle** is the best or choice example of what is available. The word is a local variant of the Scots *wale*, which comes from the Old Norse *val* a choice or selection.

wyme The **wyme** is a Northeastern name for the belly or stomach. The term is a local form of the Scots *wame*, which comes from the same source as *womb*.

wynd (rhymes with *find*) A **wynd** is a narrow street or lane, often a winding one, which leads off a larger or more important street: *the wynds, courts and closes of the Royal Mile*. **Wynd** is often used in the names of streets, such as *St Mary's Wynd* or *Kirk Wynd*.

yatter To **yatter** or **yatter on** is to talk or chatter, usually incessantly: *I could hear them yatterin away, but didn't pay any attention to what they were saying; What's he yatterin on about now?* The word is onomatopoeic.

ye Ye means you.

yellow-yite or **yite** A **yellow-yite** is a yellowhammer.

yestreen (pronounced *yes-treen*) Yestreen means last night, or sometimes, more loosely, yesterday: *It was gey wet yestreen.* The term is a contraction of **yester-**, as in yesterday, plus *even* evening.

yett A **yett** is a gate: *the prison yett; as daft as a yett on a windy day.* In place names such as *the Yetts o Muckhart*, a **yett** is a pass running between hills. **Yett** is an Old English variant of *gate*.

yeukie (pronounced *yuck-ee* or *yook-ee*) or **yokie** (pronounced *yoke-ee*) Something, such as a part of the body, that is **yeukie**, is itchy. The word comes from the Middle Dutch *jeuken* to itch, which is ultimately from the same Germanic origin as "itch".

yin Yin is a word meaning one. It is more widespread in its distribution than either **ane** or **wan**, being used in most of Scotland with the exception of the North: *Let's see the ither yin again; yin o life's great mysteries; Youse yins will have tae wait.*

yirdit Yirdit is a Northeastern word meaning dirty. It is derived from *yird*, a Scots word for earth.

yite or **yitie** Same as **yellow-yite**.

yoke To **yoke** or **yoke to** is to start work for the day (or shift): *Are you no yokit yet?* This now chiefly Northeastern term alludes to a horse being yoked up to a plough.

yokie (pronounced *yoke-ee*) A Northeastern form of **yeukie**.

yokin time Yokin time is a now chiefly Northeastern way of referring to the time when a period of work starts: *He was still in his bed come yokin time.*

yon Yon means that or those: *Whit has yon bunch o wasters ever done for us?; one of yon fancy foreign lagers.* Yon can also mean that one or those ones: *Yon's a fool.*

yon time In the Glasgow area, **yon time** is a way of referring to any unspecified but very late time: *If we miss this bus we'll not be home till yon time.*

youse or **yous** (pronounced *use* or *yiz*) Youse is a form of you sometimes used in Central Scotland when addressing or referring to more than one person: *I know youse two are lesbians; It's the moment yous have all been waitin for.* In very broad Scots it is sometimes also used as a singular: *If youse were a decent Presbyterian.*

yowe (rhymes with *now*) A yowe is a female adult sheep, a ewe: *a park o breedin yowes wi lambs.*

yumyum (pronounced *yum-yum*) A **yumyum** is a type of cake like a sausage-shaped doughnut, often with a twist in the middle of it.

Zetland Zetland is a former official name for **Shetland**. Like **Shetland**, **Zetland** comes from the Old Norse name for the islands, *Hjaltland*.